EFFECTIVE COUNSELING APPROACHES

FOR CHEMICAL ABUSERS & OFFENDERS

Gregory L. Little, ED.D., LPC

Kenneth D. Robinson, ED.D., CPC

Katherine D. Burnette, M.S., LADAC

D0066870

EAGLE WING BOOKS, INC.
P. O. Box 9972
Memphis, TN 38190

EFFECTIVE COUNSELING APPROACHES
FOR CHEMICAL ABUSERS & OFFENDERS

Published by
Eagle Wing Books, Inc.
P.O. Box 9972
Memphis, TN 38190

ISBN: 0-940829-19-3

Retail price: $12.00

DEDICATION

We don't ask for prosperity, or security; only for a reasonable chance to live, to work out our destiny in peace and decency.
George Wald

Blessed influence of one true loving human soul on another.
George Eliot — *Janet's Repentance*

Thou wert my guide, philosopher, and friend.
Pope — *Essay on Man*

This book is dedicated to

MOSE HART, JR.

A brave, caring, wise counselor who overcame seemingly insurmountable odds. His kind acts and deep understanding live on in thousands of former addicts and offenders.

TABLE OF CONTENTS

Chapter 3

Chapter 4

Chapter 5

Chapter 6

CHAPTER 1
INTRODUCTION:
History of Counseling &
Substance Abuse Counseling

Until fairly recently, alcoholism and drug abuse were regarded in the
United States as sins or crimes unrelated to any concept of mental
health or mental illness. ... Since about 1950, educated laymen, aware
that the alcoholic or drug addict suffers from impaired personal and
interpersonal functioning, have also come to look at them as sicknesses.
Bertram Brown — *Comprehensive Textbook of Psychiatry* — *II* **(1975)**

Many counselors, including chemical dependency counselors, are unfamiliar with the history of their profession, often assuming that counseling started as a branch of psychology. Counseling is more closely allied with education, albeit counseling has borrowed techniques from psychology. The purpose of this introductory section is to give readers a brief historical review of counseling and to lead readers to the understanding that the field of chemical dependency counseling remains in its infancy.

The origins of counseling in the United States as a profession can be traced to the rudimentary beginnings of community/school guidance in Vienna, Austria in 1922. Alfred Adler, a physician interested in Freudian Psychoanalysis, made a break from Freud in 1912. Adler viewed growth and development as a life-long process during which all individuals strive to become superior — that is, Adler believed that people constantly moved toward achieving goals they had consciously or unconsciously set for themselves in an attempt to become better or more efficient in a social world. Adler's theoretical position is known as *Individual Psychology*.

Adler recognized that schools and teachers were in a unique position to assist children to develop in positive ways. In an article Adler published in *The Journal of Individual Psychology* in 1930, he stated:

"The only question that remains is how we can choose the best point of attack, what method we are to find to develop children so that they can stand the tasks and problems of later life. There is a way which is practical and promises a real solution. We can make teachers the instruments of our social progress: we can train our teachers to correct mistakes made in the family, to develop and spread the social interest of the children towards others. This is an entirely natural development of the school. Because the family is not able to bring up the children for all the tasks of later life, mankind has established schools as the prolonged arm of the family. Why should we not use the school to make mankind more sociable, more cooperative, and more interested in human welfare? ... We have established Advisory Councils in the schools where the teachers can discuss with an expert the problems of the children in their class ..."

Adler is credited with developing the first intake question-naires for children and families, the use of family interviews and family therapy, and developing a therapy team including the teacher, parents, and guidance counselor. Adler recommended "guidance and counseling" for students and expanded the role of school guidance personnel. Initially, most guidance counselors were experienced teachers. Starting in the mid 1900s, some teachers received addi-tional academic training, often receiving a master's degree in guid-ance counseling or student personnel services. Adler's work contrib-uted to the expansion of counselors' roles from schools to the reha-bilitation of drug addicts, criminal populations, and the provision of occupational guidance. In America, the Adlerian movement for child guidance and counseling was championed by Rudolph Dreikurs who also advocated counseling in groups, role playing, marriage counseling, and the use of multiple counselors in various therapeutic situations. Dreikurs began pushing an Adlerian-based counseling approach in the early 1940s and began the first Adlerian Institute in Chicago.

Adler's contributions to counseling and psychology are usually unrecognized. Adler coined the terms inferiority and supe-riority complex as well as the concepts of life style and goal orientation. Also, he was the first to recognize and formulate a method to treat dependency and over-protection. Maslow's humanism, existen-tialism, Rational-Emotive Therapy, Gestalt Therapy, transactional analysis, family therapy, reality therapy, and logotherapy all borrow from Adlerian concepts.

THE ADVENT OF HUMANISM AND CLIENT-CENTERED COUNSELING:
Counseling Adopts A Method From Psychology

While psychoanalysis (Freudian Therapy) dominated psychology, many guidance counselors and some psychologists treating school-age children in the 1930s and 1940s became disenchanted with the empirical and "clinical" emphasis dominating the field. Humanism, an approach that stresses understanding, personal freedom and responsibility, and an underlying need for the individual to "self-actualize" — to realize one's potentials — rapidly gained proponents during that period. In 1938 a clinical psychologist, Carl Rogers, began to develop what he termed "nondirective" counseling at Ohio State University. In 1951 Rogers began to call the method "client-centered therapy" or "person-centered" therapy. The method was distinguished by outcome research done primarily on students and the "therapeutic relationship" between client-therapist which is characterized by a warm, accepting, trusting environment that facilitates understanding (Rogers, 1975). Rogers found that the approach had effective applications in educational settings and with other human problems. Rogers' 1942 book, *Counseling and Psychotherapy*, is still considered a major pivotal work because it showed that therapy outcomes could be measured and researched and demonstrated that the relationship and attitudes of the counselor were important in affecting treatment outcome (Goldenberg, 1973). Rogers' method produced a revolutionary change in the training of counselors and was rapidly adopted as the preferred counseling approach. Meador (1973) wrote:

"The theoretical base of client centered therapy is a belief in the 'exquisite rationality' of human growth under optimal conditions. The actualizing tendency in man is a powerful force equipped with its own power and direction.

The task of the therapist is to facilitate the client's awareness of and trust in his own actualizing processes. The primary discovery of client-centered therapy is that the attitudes of the therapist which create the optimal climate in which the client can allow his own growth to unfold. ... The attitude of uncompromising trust in the growth processes of individuals is as much a value system as it is a guide for therapy."

Client-centered therapy quickly became the primary therapeutic method in counseling departments and in guidance counselor training. The approach yielded impressive results — especially with student populations. In *An Introduction To Clinical Psychology* (1948) Pennington and Berg stated:

> "Evidence is now being accumulated as to the appropriate use of the client-centered method. Its most obvious area of applicability has been with college students. These clients usually meet the prerequisites for counseling which Rogers previously proposed, i.e., adequate intelligence, emotional freedom from family, ... and in most cases a desire for help. ... Client-centered therapy seems also to have a useful role in the counseling of marital adjustment problems. ... The method has also more applicability to the area of vocational counseling than is frequently realized. ... Another area in which the method has been used successfully is in counseling parent-child problems. ... The client-centered method has wide application to the treatment of emotional problems of normal persons and the mildly psychoneurotic" (p. 548).

The influence of client-centered therapy on counseling and counselor training is hard to overstate. The client-centered approach was found to be a unique and very positive approach that led to a vast improvement over the simple use of interest inventories and career guidance. The vast majority of counseling departments adapted the method as the primary therapeutic approach in which school/ guidance, and community counselors were trained.

THE ROOTS OF COUNSELING

Many counselors assume that their field developed as a branch from psychology. However, as discussed above, the counseling profession's *academic* beginnings actually emerged from educational guidance/vocational counseling. It is important to remember that the methods employed in counseling have traditionally been adapted from psychology, especially client-centered and humanistic philosophies.

The 1958 National Defense Education Act (NDE) was a major impetus leading to the rapid rise of departments of guidance/counseling in colleges. States were required to develop criteria allowing schools to receive federal funds to place qualified trained guidance counselors in positions and thousands were subsequently trained. Prior to the 1958 NDE Act, schools tended to utilize teachers as guidance counselors. In the late 1970s and early 1980s, student populations fell and the need for new guidance counselors waned. During that time, academic departments of counseling began expanding their course offerings and specializations — including substance abuse counseling and offender rehabilitation counseling. In 1973 a national certification for rehabilitation counselors was established (Bradley, 1991). It was during this time period that the counseling field moved from an educational orientation to a larger community focus.

Historically and currently, the gap between psychology and counseling remains. The American Personnel and Guidance Association, also known as the *American Counseling Association*, was founded in 1952, and was the primary organization to which most counselors belonged. In 1983, the organization's name was changed to The *American Association for Counseling and Development* (AACD). AACD is the overseer of the American Counseling Association (ACA). In 1996, the ACA had nearly 60,000 members. The ACA has a humanistic orientation. The Preamble to the organization's *Code Of Ethics and Standards of Practice* reads: "The American Counseling Association is an educational, scientific and professional organization whose members are dedicated to the enhancement of human development throughout the life span. Association members recognize diversity in our society and embrace a cross-cultural approach in support of the worth, dignity, potential, and uniqueness of each individual" (ACA, 1996).

Clinical psychology traces its roots to the opening of the first psychological clinic at the University of Pennsylvania in 1896 when Lightner Witmer coined the term clinical psychology. At that time, many psychologists were interested in tests and measurements utilizing the first intelligence tests and personality measures (Goldenberg, 1973) and in understanding and treating pathological behavior. Counselors, at least those who were academically trained, have been traditionally trained in counseling departments within schools of education while psychology departments were separate entities within universities' Arts and Sciences division. Large colleges and universities today tend to maintain counseling and psychology within separate departments, however, with the emergence of "counseling psychology" in the late 1970s and 1980s, and in smaller schools, the lines between the two fields have become less distinctive.

EMERGENCE OF COUNSELOR LICENSURE/CERTIFICATION

"Turf" battles occasionally erupt between psychologists and counselors with the focus often being the ability of counselors to utilize certain tests and measurements, diagnose, bill third parties for services, and treat certain disorders. These disagreements over "limits of practice" have led to credentialing — the licensing and certification of various types of counselors. The history of counselor licensure and certification began in the early 1970s. In 1972 the Board of Psychological Examiners in Virginia was granted a court restraining order stopping a counselor from conducting career counseling in a private practice because the counselor was "practicing psychology" without being licensed. The counselor argued in court that psychology and personnel and guidance counseling were separate professions and, therefore, his practice should not be subject to the regulations governing psychologists. The court ruled in late 1972 that guidance counseling and psychology were indeed separate professions, but that since counseling utilized some methods of psychology and there was no regulatory body to govern the profession of counseling, that counselors appeared to be governed by the regulations covering psychologists. The counselor was essentially banned from practicing as a counselor (Bradley, 1991).

The Virginia Personnel and Guidance Association successfully lobbied the state to pass legislation in 1975 establishing counseling as a separate profession from psychology and in 1976 Virginia began licensing counselors. Since that time, a majority of states have followed suit with licensure/certifications for substance abuse counselors emerging during the same time period. Most of the current battles over limits of practice (again, typically disagreements about diagnosis, treatment, billing, and use of tests) are settled by boards and committees within states rather than in courts. In most states, the laws outlining the practice of Licensed Professional Counselors (LPC) tend to restrict counseling to areas of antisocial behavior and normal emotional problems (as opposed to treating psychopathology). LPCs typically have at least a master's degree in counseling and additional training and experience. The requirements for substance abuse counselor certification vary widely from state to state ranging from no certification or recognition of the profession to licensure requiring some college classes and documented experience.

Clinical psychologists trained in APA *(American Psychological Association)* approved programs maintain a "scientist-practitioner" model and are trained in utilizing various personality measures, intelligence tests, and diagnostic tools in an effort to better diagnose and treat. Counseling departments are approved today by CACREP (Council for Accreditation of Counseling and Related Education Programs), an affiliate of ACA. It should be noted that prior to the establishment of CACREP in 1981, the only organization that approved most counseling departments was the National Council for Accreditation of Teacher Education.

Clinical psychologists may receive a Ph.D. in psychology or a Psy.D. Counselors can receive a Ph.D. in counseling or counseling psychology or an Ed.D. in counseling. School or educational psychologists can receive Ph.D. or Ed.D. degrees depending on the department and school (Ed.S. degrees are also available). In addition, both departments offer various masters degrees including M.S., M.A., and M.Ed. With a few narrow exceptions, all 50 states legally restrict the use of the term "psychologist" to those who have a doctorate in the field and a license. In 1994, 41 states and the District of Columbia had established counselor licensure, certification, or a registry system. The American Counseling Association is a prime mover in attempting to have all states adopt a uniform system of counselor licensure or certification. A similar push has occurred with licensure or certification for substance abuse counselors. NAADAC (National Association of Alcoholism and Drug Abuse Counselors) has established standards that have become the model for states initiating licensure/certification laws for drug/alcohol counselors.

SUBSTANCE ABUSE /OFFENDER COUNSELING

In 1976 the senior author of this text received a master's degree in experimental psychology from Memphis State University (now the University of Memphis). In 1977, he entered the doctoral counseling program housed in the university's School of Education and subsequently received an Ed.D. (Doctor of Education) in counseling. He made this move, in part, because he had began a career as a drug counselor within a local prison as a summer job but had become the program director nine months later. The drug program he directed was a behavioristic therapeutic community and he had been trained in behaviorism at the master's level. But the counseling department's program was characterized by its strong emphasis on client-centered counseling and the humanistic philosophy. Two types of counselors were trained in the department at that time: school guidance counselors (the majority of the students) and "community agency" counselors. Other than client centered approaches, at that time there were no other therapeutic approaches taught in the department until the first behaviorally-oriented faculty was hired a year later. One course in substance abuse counseling was taught. Nearly a decade later a master's degree in substance abuse counseling was offered and a counseling psychology program was developed in the late 1980s.

Substance abuse counseling as a profession emerged in the 1960s and 1970s during the rapid rise of drug use in that era. Most colleges developed a few courses in drug abuse and academic training for the field was provided primarily by counseling departments, social work, or departments of "human relations." The emphasis on client-centered counseling for substance abuse remains today. For example, in 1990-1993 the senior author of this text taught in Shelby State Community College's Substance Abuse Counselor Technical Certification Program. In one course the text, *Essentials of Chemical Dependency Counseling* (Lawson, Ellis, & Rivers, 1984), was employed. The text stresses trust, acceptance, reflecting feelings, restating content, developing and fostering empathy, and clarifying client statements. These are, of course, the primary elements of client-centered counseling. The text did not refer to a single outcome study indicating that these techniques actually worked as a substance abuse treatment, it simply assumed that they are essential techniques. Substance abuse counselor licensure / certification tests stress these techniques and counselors should be knowledgeable of them. For example, NAADAC standards (those which many states use for their testing requirements prior to granting of a license or certificate) include knowledge of feedback, attending, paraphrasing and restating, reflection of feelings, and the development of trust.

For many reasons addressed later in this text, substance abuse counseling and offender counseling/rehabilitation are gradually overlapping. Substantial research has been accumulated on appropriate therapeutic approaches with offenders who abuse substances and today, many programs are required by their funding sources to utilize methods with proven effectiveness. For example, cognitive skills and cognitive-behavioral methods are very frequently called for in grant proposals. Many substance abuse counselors find these treatment requirements surprising when they treat substance abusers from criminal justice. For example, many programs in criminal justice today are behaviorally oriented with little emphasis placed on developing a warm, trusting relationship with the client.

Criminal justice researchers have the means to reliably and validly calculate the effectiveness of therapeutic approaches on offenders by analyzing the recidivism of treated offenders. Rearrests, convictions, parole/probation violations, and job status are available on offenders and have all been used as outcome measures. Andrews (1994) reported on several meta-analyses of treatment interventions with offenders covering over 1,000 separate outcome studies. In his section titled "What Doesn't Work," "non-directive client-centered counseling" is cited as ineffective. Gendreau (1995), reporting on data from numerous meta-analyses of treatment outcomes with offenders, lists as "Ineffective Interventions" psychodynamic approaches and "Rogerian" non-directive or client-centered therapies. Numerous other reviews of the published outcome literature have reached the same conclusion (see Little & Robinson, 1997). Thus, at least in treating substance abusers from criminal justice, counselors should be aware that many of the most respected treatment researchers reject the use of individual client-centered approaches.

Today, "counselors" are trained in a variety of departments in both the community college and university level. A bewildering variety of technical certificates and degrees are offered ranging from below associates degree level through doctorates.

HISTORY OF DRUG TREATMENT

In 1940, Professor Alfred Lindesmith of Indiana University wrote: "The treatment of addicts in the United States today is on no higher plane than the persecution of witches of other ages, and like the latter it is to be hoped that it will soon become merely another dark chapter of history." In 1957, psychiatrist Karl Bowman wrote, "Our whole dealing with the problem of drug addiction for the past 40 years has been a sorry mess." Biochemist Robert de Ropp wrote in 1957, "Just why the alcoholic is tolerated as a sick man while the opiate addict is persecuted as a criminal is hard to understand." The American Medical Association and American Bar Association delivered a joint statement in 1958: "In the first place it is doubtful whether drug addicts can be deterred from using drugs by threats of jail or prison sentences. The belief that fear of punishment is a vital factor in deterring an addict from using drugs rests upon a superficial view of the drug addiction process and the nature of drug addiction..." (Brecher, 1972).

The passage of the Harrison Drug Act in 1914 is considered by many to be the starting point in the "treatment" of addicts (Drug Abuse Survey Project, 1977). Treatment, in this case, meant separation of the addict from the widely available drugs — mainly opiates. In 1918 the Treasury Department found in a survey that 73,150 addicts were being supplied narcotics by the 31% of all physicians who answered the survey. Shortly after 1918, 40 narcotic maintenance clinics were opened by cities in the United States to legally provide narcotics to addicts. This represented the beginning of efforts similar to modern drug maintenance programs. But the Narcotic Division of the Treasury Department struck back by arresting 25,000 doctors who had dispensed narcotics between 1914 and 1938 actually sending 5,000 of them to jail. In 1935-1938, the U.S. Public Health Service established clinics to treat addicts going to federal prisons at Fort Worth, TX and Lexington, KY. The treatment philosophy was simple; take the drugs away, let them go through withdrawal, and send them back home when their sentence was completed. It was not until around the late 1950s that it was recognized that this approach didn't work (DeLong, 1972).

In 1959 the first drug therapeutic community (TC), Synanon, was established in an attempt to "restructure the addict's character." By 1969, 183 TCs were established in the states. Some refer to the TC as "milieu therapy," an approach widely used in hospitals prior to the first drug TC (Freedman, Kaplan, & Sadock, 1975).

The Federal Bureau of Prisons subsequently established TCs

in several federal prisons while the TC model began operating in numerous local and state facilities. By the early 1980s the TCs had been eliminated in Federal prisons, but the model remained active in several state and local prisons and rehabilitation programs (DeLong, 1972). TCs, and other similar residential drug rehabilitation programs, today treat the entire range of chemical dependency problems including alcohol, opiates, cocaine, and other drugs. Numerous states operate TCs in prisons with offenders who abuse drugs and currently there is a push by many states to establish TCs in prisons.

Methadone maintenance was begun in 1964 by Vincent Dole and today is considered to be a successful approach in treating narcotic (opiate) addiction. Methadone maintenance clinics serve more patients than any other formal treatment approach.

Beginning in the late 1960s, community-based programs began substantial treatment efforts utilizing various counseling approaches on both an inpatient and outpatient basis. While most of these programs defined themselves as "halfway houses" or rehabilitation centers, they combined group and individual counseling with support groups. Until the early 1980s, addiction counselors were often "in recovery" themselves or were trained by counseling or related academic departments. Treatment approaches and philosophies borrowed heavily from the medical model of alcoholism treatment.

Most programs today identify themselves as *"multimodal"* employing combinations of group counseling, individual counseling, drug and alcohol education, family counseling, drug usage screenings, vocational/educational support, and utilizing self-help 12-step support groups like AA, NA, or CA. This approach, recognizing the "disease concept" of addiction, is referred to by some as the "Traditional Model." Many other programs have a strongly behavioristic overlay with a rigid structure, sanctions for rule violations, and rewards for compliance. TCs are expanding, especially within criminal justice. Most drug treatment programs (including TCs) that treat offenders also utilize approaches identified as "social skills," cognitive-behavioral treatment, Moral Reconation Therapy ® (a cognitive-behavioral system), behavior management, Rational-Emotive Therapy, Reality Therapy, Rational-Behavior Therapy, or social learning approaches.

HISTORY OF ALCOHOL TREATMENT:
Traditional Chemical Dependency Treatment — the Minnesota Model

The history of alcohol treatment extends far into antiquity with primarily legal and moral approaches dominating until the mid-1900s. A combination of events led to the development of AA and a revolutionary approach to alcoholism in the late 1930s.

Psychologist Carl Jung treated a Roland H. for alcoholism in the early 1930s and, after Roland relapsed, Jung stated to his patient that only a spiritual experience could save him. Roland subsequently attended meetings of an evangelical group that had developed a spiritual approach to alcoholism and personal conduct. After attending meetings of the "Oxford Movement" Roland stopped drinking. Roland, in turn, introduced another alcoholic named Ebby to the Oxford meetings which were based upon "Buchmanism" (named after its founder Frank Buchman who initiated his group movement in the late 1910s). In 1938, Buchman renamed his Oxford movement Moral ReArmament (MRA®), but during the interim, Ebby had introduced another alcoholic, Bill Wilson, to Oxford meetings. Wilson, in turn, introduced Dr. Bob Smith to Oxford Groups. Wilson and Dr. Smith began writing the *Alcoholics Anonymous Big Book* in 1938, distilling the essential principles of Buchmanism into 12 Steps. In April 1939 the first AA *Big Book* was printed with 5,000 copies. It is believed that Wilson's fledgling AA had about 100 members at that time. In the early 1990s, about 2,000,000 people worldwide attended AA meetings (Bufe, 1991).

In 1949, Hazelden (of Minnesota) began publishing books and educational materials in support of AA concepts. During the same period, Dr. E. M. Jellinek researched alcoholism and formulated the medical-disease concept of alcoholism. Jellinek formally promoted the "medical-model" in the early 1960s and it was immediately embraced by AA and eventually by medical organizations.

Many drug treatment programs employ what is sometimes termed the *Traditional Chemical Dependency Treatment* approach — also called the Minnesota Model. The Minnesota model "generally involves medically supervised detoxification in combination with a range of biopsychosocial treatment services. This approach emphasizes addiction as a disease and encourages participation in a 12-Step program" (SAMHSA, 1996).

The traditional model is not without detractors — a fact that chemical dependency counselors need to recognize. Many alcohol and substance abuse counselors work within agencies and programs that utilize the Minnesota model and skepticism over program treatment claims are frequent. It is notable that relatively few programs within criminal justice utilize the approach today. On November 9, 1993, the Minneapolis-St. Paul *Press Journal* published an analysis by insurance companies on Minnesota programs using the Minnesota Model. The state provided data showing that 30,000 Minnesotans entered "traditional" Minnesota Model substance abuse programs each year, but two-thirds of the clients had been in treatment before. More than half were in their 3rd, 4th, or 5th treatment. Programs claimed a 60%-70% success rate in keeping addicts or alcoholics clean for six to 12 months after treatment. However, the short-term abstinence rate was actually found to be less than 50% while long-term abstinence was only 10% to 30%. The article stated: "The National Academy of Sciences and Institute of Medicine concluded in 1990 that the Minnesota model has the highest revenues, the second largest number of clients (methadone programs were first) and the smallest scientific basis for measuring effectiveness of any substance abuse treatment method." The article goes on to state that "The success rates they (the programs) do claim are often exaggerated. ... This is a disturbing state of affairs for an industry so deeply entrenched and widely copied."

CHEMICAL ABUSE COUNSELING IS IN ITS INFANCY

While many in the treatment field don't realize it, it is important to recognize that chemical dependency treatment remains in its infancy. Despite the fact that thousands of research studies have been conducted, we have yet to establish exactly which types of programs work best for which types of clients. In addition, we should understand that many professionals are skeptical of the benefits of treatment. Even treatment specialists cannot agree. Arguments persist over the use of aversion therapy, controlled drinking, behavioral approaches, the disease concept, and even the effects of 12-Step programs. Relapse prevention is partly an outgrowth of some of the controlled drinking studies in the 1970s, and actually has scant data supporting the effectiveness of the approach. Psychopharmacological approaches, even when data shows they effectively aid those in recovery, are resisted by many treatment professionals. In coming years we will see new methodologies employed in the field including vaccinations for cocaine abusers, synthetic antibodies, and chemical blockers. We have to keep in mind that chemical abuse counseling is a developing field and that our treatment technologies and approaches can and should improve. Thus, it is wise for counselors to keep current on innovations and treatment improvements. In the final paragraph of the final chapter in the text *Psychopharmacology* (Little, 1997) it is stated:

> "It's also wise to be open and scientifically honest about new treatment strategies and the effectiveness of the ones we already have. One basic difference between counselors and neuroscientists is in their scientific philosophy about failure. We counselors tend to blame our clients for their treatment failures. Psychopharmacologists treating disorders blame ineffective treatments. They are constantly looking for improved methods, procedures, and treatment interventions and are patient and confident about coming improvements. Perhaps we can take a clue from this outlook" (p. 255).

WHAT THE CHEMICAL DEPENDENCY (CD) COUNSELOR NEEDS TO KNOW ABOUT COUNSELING TECHNIQUES

Most states licensing or certifying CD counselors require counselors to be "familiar with" or have a "working knowledge of" at least three different counseling approaches. While the choices of the three methods are up to the individual, in reality, one of those should be Client-Centered Therapy. The reason for this is simple. National and state tests ask questions about restatement, reflection of feelings, empathy, and other Client-Centered concepts. These concepts and methods often form the underlying basis for other counseling techniques and are an essential foundation. In addition, the underlying philosophy of the Client-Centered approach certainly promotes many desirable and effective counselor traits. Thus, following a brief introduction to defense mechanisms and basic counseling knowledge, Client-Centered Counseling is covered first.

It is a purpose of this text to provide chemical dependency counselors a "working knowledge" of the theories of counseling most frequently employed. A basic knowledge of each theory is covered in separate chapters, and sufficient information is presented to obtain an elementary level of knowledge sufficient for most tests. However, it should be understood that more in-depth study and supervised practice should be performed prior to utilizing any of the techniques and theories presented.

The primary approaches that will be covered in this text are Client-Centered Counseling, Reality Therapy, Rational-Emotive Therapy, Behavior Therapy, Cognitive-Behavioral Therapy, Gestalt, and Transactional Analysis. A brief discussion of group applications of methods will be briefly addressed in some chapters.

One other issue regarding substance abuse counseling should be addressed. Many counselors consider themselves to be "eclectic." An eclectic counselor is one who has mastered several treatment approaches and systems. Eclectic counseling involves the ability of the treatment professional to recognize which treatment system should be used for the client or the presenting problem. For instance, a counselor treating someone who is experiencing grief may use the Client-centered approach with that client while choosing to employ cognitive-behavioral techniques for a client who is a substance abuser. Another view of eclectic counseling is the treatment professional who uses bits and pieces from different treatment systems within a single session to treat the client or the presenting problem. While practicing within the scope of the second view of eclectic counseling, the treatment professional needs to possess knowledge and expertise in a wide variety of therapeutic techniques and theories.

Eclectic counselors do not exclusively use one set of treatment strategies or approaches. Some believe that eclectic counseling is a "jack-of-all-trades-master-of-none" approach (Linden, 1984; Russell, 1986). In order to make the claim of being a competent eclectic counselor, the professional must maintain a level of expertise and remain up to date in all therapeutic systems. Therefore, it may not be wise for a substance abuse counselor, taking an oral exam or making a case presentation, to make the claim of being an eclectic counselor.

CHAPTER 2
CHEMICAL ABUSE COUNSELING:
Definitions, Goals, & Basics

Clients come for help because they have crises, troubles, doubts, difficulties, frustrations, or concerns. These are often called, generically, "problems," but they are not problems in a mathematical sense, because emotions run high and often there are no clear-cut solutions. It is probably better to say that clients come, not with problems, but with *problem situations*.
Gerald Egan — *The Skilled Helper* (1990)

Counseling tends to mean different things to different people and, as a result, many different definitions exist. "There are numerous schools, models, and methods of counseling, and theoretical assumptions and definitions of what constitutes counseling, each with its own techniques. ... Counseling involves a therapeutic relationship between a counselor ... and a drug client. Ideally, it is a relationship built upon mutual trust, respect, and understanding. It is a goal-oriented endeavor based upon a treatment plan that recognizes both the internal psychological struggles (of the user) ... as well as the impact of societal demands upon the client. Within the supporting milieu and warmth of this relationship, the client derives nourishment and becomes motivated toward health and adjustment. Through support, guidance, and identification with the counselor, (the user) can relinquish drug abuse, move on to function in a more socially acceptable way, and learn to realize his or her potential in education, job, and career" (Marks, Daroff, & Granick, 1985).

Corey (1977) defines counseling as *"the process whereby clients are afforded the opportunity to explore personal concerns; this exploration leads to an increase of awareness and of choice possibilities."* Another basic definition of counseling is, "Counseling is the process by which a counselor assists a client to face, understand, and accept information about himself and his interactions with others, so that he can make effective decisions about various life choices" (Cottle & Downie, 1970). Regarding substance abuse counseling, most professionals agree that *counseling involves a therapeutic relationship in which the counselor serves to help clients mobilize their resources to solve their chemical abuse problems by examining and modifying attitudes, values, feelings, and behaviors.*

CHEMICAL ABUSE COUNSELING TASKS & GOALS

"The specific counseling approach or methods used in individual treatment of substance abusers come from modalities originally developed to treat other conditions. Regardless of the particular counseling model endorsed, there are some tasks or goals of individual treatment that usually are seen across all approaches, although the emphasis placed on each may vary. These include (Rounsaville & Carroll, 1992):

• helping the individual resolve to stop using psychoactive substances;

• teaching coping skills to help the person avoid relapse after achieving an initial period of abstinence;

• changing reinforcement contingencies;

• fostering management of painful feelings; and

• improving interpersonal functioning and enhancing social supports.

Substance abusers typically enter treatment with the goal of controlled use, especially of alcohol. Therapists help patients explore their motivation and set appropriate treatment goals, including a goal of abstinence. Identifying circumstances that increase the likelihood of resuming drug use and practicing strategies for coping with these high risk situations are other parts of the treatment process. For many substance abusers, drug use has been the entire focus of their lives. When it stops, they need help in filling their time and finding rewards that replace those derived from drug use. Many drug-involved persons have never achieved satisfactory adult relationships or vocational skills because drug abuse was initiated during adolescence or early adult years. Individual interventions can help them maintain their motivation during the processes of learning new skills and recovery. Individual therapy often includes techniques to elicit strong feelings and help the individual learn acceptable means of managing them within the protected environment of the therapeutic setting. For some persons who have emotional or anxiety disorders, combined treatment with medications and individual counseling may be appropriate. Encouraging the person to participate in self-help groups can provide a source of social support outside of individual counseling sessions" (Crowe, & Reeves, 1994).

GROUP COUNSELING

While this is not a text on group counseling, substance abuse counselors preparing to take licensure/certification tests should be knowledgeable of how individual counseling approaches can be utilized in group formats. Sadock (Freedman, Kaplan, & Sadock, 1975) defines group therapy as *"a form of treatment in which carefully selected ... persons are placed into a group, guided by a trained therapist, for the purpose of helping one another effect personality change. By means of a variety of technical maneuvers and theoretical constructs, the leader uses the group members' interactions to bring about this change"* (p. 1850).

Group therapy is often combined with other treatment modalities to provide a structured, comprehensive treatment program for substance abusers. Washton (1992, p. 508) defines group therapy as: *"... an assembly of chemically dependent patients, usually five to ten in number, who meet regularly (usually at least once a week) under the guidance of a professional leader (usually a professional therapist or addiction counselor) for the purpose of promoting abstinence from all mood-altering chemicals and recovery from addiction."*

The treatment goals of group therapy may include (Washton, 1992):

- establishing abstinence;
- integration of the individual into the group;
- stabilization of individual functioning;
- relapse prevention; and
- identifying and working through long-standing problems that have been obscured or exacerbated by substance abuse (Crowe & Reeves, 1994).

Several types of groups exist (Crowe & Reeves, 1994). These include:

- *Exploratory groups* where members' feelings are explored and interpreted. The goal is often to assist members in developing the ability to tolerate distressing feelings without resorting to chemicals.
- *Supportive groups* that assist members in adjusting to absti-

nence by helping them identify and use resources and provide motivation to remain abstinent.

- *Interaction groups* where an atmosphere of trust and safety create a cohesive group so that members can share in-depth self-disclosure.

- *Interpersonal problem solving groups* where programs may use the group to resolve interpersonal problems and difficulties among group members; and where members can learn appropriate techniques of problem solving in a sequential process: problem recognition, problem definition, generating possible solutions, selecting best alternatives.

- *Educational groups* where specific information on relevant issues are presented followed by discussion.

- *Structured cognitive-behavioral groups* following a sequential, task-oriented process focused on specific areas; i.e., relapse prevention, anger management, job readiness, etc.

COUNSELING IN THE TREATMENT PROCESS

Counseling is one (perhaps the most important) component in the overall treatment process. *The specific strategy a counselor will use on a particular client should ideally be matched to the needs of the client and the resources of the program.* Programs that treat all of their clients according to a single philosophy and approach should, at the least, maintain working agreements with other agencies that can meet client needs not addressed by the program's treatment approach. "Treatment is an effective tool in reducing drug abuse and rehabilitating those affected by it. It is particularly important that treatment strategies incorporate the five critical components to enhance effectiveness" (Crowe & Reeves, 1994). The five sequential treatment components are:

1. **Assessment** using diagnostic tools and structured interview processes to determine an individual's needs and problems. Assessments may diagnose other disorders co-occurring with chemical abuse problems. Although assessments are often done by counselors, the assessment stage is considered to be preliminary to counseling itself.

2. **Patient-Treatment Matching** that ensures the client will receive specific treatments in accordance with patient personality,

background, mental condition, and the extent and duration of chemical abuse. During this stage of treatment, a preliminary treatment plan is typically formed as a joint effort between the client and counselor or treatment team.

3. Comprehensive Services include the full range of services needed for a patient including specific chemical abuse treatment. Counseling as a formal process typically begins in this stage. Client needs that may be addressed include health problems, financial/legal issues, psychological issues, social support, family problems, educational/vocational issues and chemical abuse.

4. Relapse Prevention may overlap the formal counseling process begun in the prior treatment stage or may be the beginning of a planned "aftercare" stage begun prior to the client's "return" to his/her community (Little, 1996). This treatment component is considered essential because addiction is a chronic, relapsing condition with predictable relapse "triggers" — specific people, places, and situations where clients are likely to relapse. These triggers can often be identified during counseling or through specific processes developed for relapse prevention approaches.

5. Accountability-Aftercare where programs assess the effectiveness of their treatment strategy and provide client support and additional services. "The need for the program, its integrity, and its results, including abstinence, social adjustment, and reduction of criminal behavior by those treated in the program, must be evaluated" (Crowe & Reeves, 1994).

ISSUES ENCOUNTERED IN MATCHING CLIENTS TO APPROPRIATE COUNSELING TECHNIQUES

A variety of possible factors can and should be considered in matching specific counseling approaches with different types of clients. In general, most chemical abuse treatment professionals believe that the more severe and longer the duration of chemical abuse, the more appropriate a client is for residential (long-term care). Counselors should be aware that a "one-size fits all" strategy for counseling approaches is rejected by most state licensing boards. This is one reason why most states require counselors to have knowledge of at least three separate counseling approaches. In addition, some clients with dual-diagnoses may need psychiatric medications while many others will be in need of basic health care. Health care and psychiatric illness can often be the most immediate needs displayed by clients and should be addressed quickly. Counselors should be aware that life-threatening issues and problems take priority, for example, suicidal depression should be treated immediately by programs.

Family Therapy. The possibility of family involvement in a client's treatment may dictate whether or not family therapy can be utilized. In addition, the presence of staff trained in appropriate family therapy methods can play an important role in this aspect of treatment. While family involvement is usually considered a desirable component of comprehensive chemical abuse treatment, some programs (e.g., criminal justice programs) may find this impractical or impossible.

Dual Diagnosis - Multiple Diagnosis. The vast majority of chemical abuse clients will have some other co-occurring diagnosis. The Regier, et. al. (1990) survey of over 20,000 residents in five states reported that 44% of alcoholics had an additional psychiatric diagnosis and 64.4% of other drug abusers had additional psychiatric diagnoses. Woody (1996) stated, "Because each dual disorder can aggravate the course of the other, both disorders must be treated." In reviewing the mass of data on alcoholics, Schuckit (1996) cites the frequent observation that about one-third of alcoholics show intense depression or severe anxiety. Drake and Mueser (1996) state that 50% of people with severe mental illness (i.e., schizophrenia, Bipolar Affective Disorder) develop alcohol or other drug use disorders. Others (Lilenfeld & Kaye, 1996) have reviewed the link between eating disorders and alcohol/drug abuse. The use of appropriate medications to treat severe psychiatric illness is essential to all substance abuse treatment programs (Little, 1997).

Personality Disorders - Offenders. Most offenders referred to chemical abuse treatment will have a *DSM-IV* Cluster B personality disorder with the majority showing Antisocial Personality Disorder (see Little & Robinson, 1997 for a review). As stated in the prior chapter, substantial outcome research exists on this subpopulation of chemical abusers. Chemical abusers who are antisocial (ASPD) tend to be highly resistant to treatment efforts and do poorly in most traditional approaches (Mathias, 1996). Behavioral and cognitive-behavioral strategies, often performed within therapeutic communities, tend to yield impressive results with such clients while client-centered approaches do not.

Many substance abuse treatment programs and agencies are experiencing an influx of such clients. Some states have seriously curtailed treatment funds (including Medicaid funding) available for substance abuse. Thus, programs searching for funding and clients have turned to criminal justice referrals and offender treatment grants to support the programs. In addition, DUI/DWI legal requirements often force such offenders into treatment. Some programs find treating clients mandated to treatment beneficial while others simply disagree preferring to treat "volunteers." SAMHSA's (1996) review of research in this area states that "Patients who are legally pressured to participate in addiction treatment: (1) have an increased likelihood of participating in treatment, (2) tend to remain in treatment longer, and (3) have similar treatment outcomes as patients who voluntarily participate."

COUNSELING INTERPERSONAL ISSUES:
The Relationship Between Counselor & Client and Treatment Effectiveness

Substantial research has been conducted on therapist characteristics and treatment outcome. "High levels of therapist empathy (understanding) are associated with positive treatment outcomes. The higher the level of counselor functioning in interpersonal skills, the better the treatment outcomes related to relapse and abstinence" (SAMHSA, 1996). The Center for Substance Abuse Treatment's (Crowe & Reeves, 1994) findings on this issue was summarized: "Staff must be firm and provide strong leadership, while showing compassion and modeling positive personal characteristics. ... Staff attitudes are also an important program factor. Permissive attitudes among staff may result in viewing society or outside forces as responsible for one's addiction. Thus, neither the staff nor the person in treatment is confronted with taking responsibility for actions to change behaviors and attitudes during treatment. ... Rather, attitudes that require responsibility and accountability may be more productive."

In summary, chemical abuse counselors should develop a warm, empathic relationship with clients and display strong, positive interpersonal skills. Staff should be cognizant of the fact that they serve as role models for clients in more ways than they might realize.

Transference

Patients develop feelings about their counselors that can relate to the patient's underlying attitudes, values, and past experiences. *Transference is the displacement of client feelings toward a counselor.* For example, some patients may come to see the counselor as a parental figure while others may develop affection. Clients enter the counseling relationship with preconceived notions about counselors, men, women, and different ethnic groups and these client beliefs can definitely affect the counseling relationship. These preconceived notions can be projected upon the counselor much like a movie is projected on a screen. The counselor serves as the screen and the client's beliefs and attitudes (preconceived notions) are the movie that gets projected.

Sometimes exploring significant events that led to a client's beliefs about their feelings can aid in "working through" transference. In general, counselors tend to be encouraged to use positive transference (when a client develops positive feelings toward the counselor) as an aid in helping clients maintain sobriety. Caution must be used in this approach — the purpose of treatment is not to make a client dependent on the counselor. It is wise for the counselor to keep in mind who is in treatment and why they are there, thus, working through transference can mean that the counselor reminds the client of the goals of treatment — that the client achieve and maintain abstinence and reach positive potentials in life.

In group therapy, transference can take on a slightly different meaning. While the group leader usually is viewed as a parental or supervisory figure, a client's feelings about significant people in their lives can transfer to other group members. Once again, group participants come together with preconceived notions. Sometimes another group member can seem like someone else who is significant in a client's life. Feelings about that significant person can be projected upon the group member. For example, a group member can seem to be "just like" a brother, parent, or former friend. When this occurs, a client will tend to express the feelings they have for that "brother, parent, or friend" onto the group member. Exploring such feelings and associations can be part of the group counseling process and form the basis of some types of groups' effectiveness.

Countertransference

Counselors develop feelings toward clients that can range from disgust to infatuation. ***Countertransference refers to the displacement of counselor feelings toward a client.*** Counselors enter the counseling relationship with preconceived notions, beliefs, attitudes, likes and dislikes that can lead to a wide range of feelings. Counselors need to remind themselves of who is in treatment and why they are there. In addition, commitments to providing ethical and nonbiased care means that adequate treatment should be provided to all clients regardless of how the counselor feels about them. Discussion of countertransference feelings with another trusted professional is often encouraged.

ESSENTIAL COUNSELOR SKILLS & BASIC ABILITIES

All substance abuse counselors need to be able to truly listen to and understand clients in both individual and group sessions. While this might seem to be a simplistic and unnecessary statement, tests and oral exams inquire how this is accomplished. Counselors must demonstrate skills in attending to clients, giving feedback, paraphrasing client statements, reflecting client feelings, self-disclosing as appropriate and necessary, confronting client behavior, and assisting clients in learning new skills. Counselors are expected to be able to adequately define each of these skills, the purposes, and how each is accomplished. While some of these are the essential core of Client-centered therapy, not all are.

Attending To Clients. Active, undivided attention to the client's verbal and nonverbal statements and actions form the core of the counseling process. You have to listen to the client, notice their reactions and gestures, and communicate to the client in various ways that you hear what they are saying. Maintaining some degree of eye contact is essential to this process, but counselors should be sensitive to the fact that continual eye contact is threatening to some cultural groups. Body posture is important and appropriately leaning toward the client at critical times demonstrates attending as does nodding, appropriate feedback, and allowing the client to finish statements without interruption or rapidly moving to other topics.

Giving Feedback. Feedback represents the counselor's responses to the client in both verbal statements and in nonverbal ways. It is designed to assist the client by letting him or her know what the counselor's observations are. Usually, feedback should be given quickly as appropriate and should be specific and non-vague. Avoid generalities with feedback and focus feedback on the client's behavior and statements rather than making judgements.

Paraphrasing Client Statements. Paraphrasing represents a restatement of what a client says, but in the counselor's own words and it sometimes highlights or focuses on important words the client uses. When a counselor paraphrases a client's statement, it lets the client know that the counselor is really hearing what they have to say and understands. Paraphrasing can clarify client statements and feelings and fosters empathy — true understanding. The act of paraphrasing in itself communicates to the client that the counselor is trying to understand and cares about what the client says — it often communicates warmth. Paraphrasing can encourage the client to go deeper and share more information. Paraphrasing can also involve feedback in that the counselor can verify if he/she understands. Asking a simple question at the end of the paraphrasing can aid the process. For example, asking, "Is that what you mean?" or "Is that correct?" are appropriate.

Reflecting Client Feelings. When counselors reflect the emotional or feeling elements of a client's statements, both verbal and nonverbal, an attempt is being made to succinctly state the deep feelings of the client. Feeling reflection is a form of feedback and is used to foster empathy and warmth — to show understanding and care/concern. Clients often view accurate reflection of their feelings by counselors as positive and enhances their ability and willingness to go deeper. It can foster a client's understanding of what is occurring within him/her at a deeper level. Counselors must first identify feelings expressed by clients in verbal statements and in other cues (body language, tone and loudness of voice, emphasis on a particular word). After the identification of the feelings, the counselor formulates a response which consists of feedback which assists the client in getting a clearer understanding of what he or she is feeling. The word "feeling" is used in the beginning of a counselor's feelings reflection. For example, the counselor might say, "You seem to be feeling..." After the statement is made, a brief question, "Is that correct?" is often posed to the client.

Counselor Self-Disclosure. Counselor self-disclosure occurs in two ways. First, counselors can tell clients how they are feeling or responding to the client's statements and feelings in the counseling process itself. This can build trust in the relationship and foster more empathy. In general, such disclosure should be done with the client's welfare in mind — when a counselor self-discloses, the focus moves to the counselor's feelings. Such disclosures are best if they are positive and beneficial and do not belittle or trivialize the client. An appropriate disclosure would be saying something like, "I'm feeling sad and angry too. It's frustrating to try to help someone and have them misunderstand so much." Second, some self-disclosures represent a counselor sharing personal information that is relevant to the client's situation. Many counselors in recovery tell clients that they, too, struggled to overcome chemical abuse. Most counselors have faced the death of a loved one or a shattered relationship. This can let a client know that their situation isn't unique and that there is hope. The purpose of such disclosures should be to assist the client and counselors are cautioned to enter self-disclosure slowly and at a point after the therapeutic relationship has developed to some extent. Counselors should share only information that is not too personal and revealing and tell clients only what they feel comfortable with. A guiding principle in self-disclosure with treating offenders has often been to assume that what you self-disclose to clients will be repeated.

Confronting Clients. Varying forms of client confrontation exist. Confrontation means that the counselor uses a statement or a question to urge the client to face a situation or behavior that appears to be avoided or ignored by the client. Confrontation raises the awareness of clients and encourages responsible behavior. Confrontation, used appropriately, can help clients see the reality of situations. Confrontations should usually be phrased as observations or questions rather than judgements or solutions. Confrontation can help clients become more "congruent" — where a client's actions and perceptions match each other. They assist clients in focusing on problem areas, reduce defenses, and accept responsibility. Counselors serve as role models and are cautioned that in a confrontation they may have incongruities pointed out to them. Client confrontations should be specific (i.e. focused on behavior, statements, or feelings), positive, and constructive in format. Confrontations that point out discrepancies or incongruities often begin with, "You say that you are..., but your actions show.... What do you think/feel that this means?"

Teaching Clients New Skills. Modern addiction treatment research has found that many clients lack basic skills in a wide range of areas. Counselors can assist clients in learning these skills by modeling, the provision of basic skills building services, exercises, or programs in educational formats. Modeling is derived from social learning concepts and teaches clients healthy and positive habits and behaviors by allowing them to observe others. As stated earlier, counselors serve as role models (as do advanced clients in some programs). Counselors should take care in serving as effective role models by showing clients appropriate interpersonal and personal behavior. Programs that maintain a therapeutic community environment use advanced clients who have demonstrated appropriate behavior as models. The use of specific audiovisual aids is often recommended. Role playing exercises also help in skills-building. Specific skills counselors can teach clients include relaxation training, assertion training, problem solving, vocational-job readiness, and conflict resolution. Relaxation training includes guided imagery, muscle relaxation, and breathing exercises that foster the client's ability to relax and handle stress. Assertion training teaches clients to be respectful of others while asserting their rights and opinions. Problem solving models typically teach clients systematic ways to troubleshoot problems by identifying the problem, considering options, and making an appropriate choice. Vocational job readiness programs teach clients appropriate job attitudes and behaviors while teaching the basics of preparing for interviews. Conflict resolution models often use a three step model: identifying the conflict, generating all options to resolve the conflict to all parties' satisfaction, and negotiating an appropriate resolution.

UNDERSTANDING DEFENSE MECHANISMS

While some counselors tend to view Freud with a degree of disdain or indifference, the concept of defense mechanisms and the formulation of each of them comes from Psychoanalysis (Freedman, Kaplan, & Sadock, 1975). Chemical abuse counselors frequently encounter denial, projection, rationalization, justification, repression, and other defense mechanisms in clients. Most clients in treatment will display more than one defense mechanism. A basic understanding of the most commonly observed defense mechanisms in chemical abuse clients is necessary, however, only a superficial and brief listing is provided here.

"Defense mechanisms are used by the ego to reduce anxiety associated with threatening situations and feelings" (Gilliland, James, & Bowman, 1994). For simplicity, the term ego means the conscious, "aware" part of the personality. Defense mechanisms tend to occur in response to inner conflict and anxiety sometimes provoked by events and situations. They are usually *unconscious* processes (that is, the client is not consciously aware of their emergence) that develop early in life as coping mechanisms. It is important to understand that simply telling a client that they are in denial won't make the denial disappear. In true denial, the client doesn't know that they are in denial. Too frequently, chemical abusing clients who deny the truth about themselves aren't using the defense mechanism of denial, they are lying. In addition, the dismantlement or smashing of all of a patient's defense mechanisms is not necessarily the goal of chemical abuse treatment. A brief summary of common defense mechanisms follows (adapted from: Chaplin, 1975; Eidelberg, 1968; Freedman, Kaplan, & Sadock, 1975; Ruch & Zimbardo, 1971; Wolman, 1973).

Denial

Denial is refusal to perceive an unpleasant reality. For example, some alcoholics who drink only beer adamantly express the idea that drinking beer cannot lead one to become an alcoholic. Denial can be thought of as an underlying fear to face the reality of a situation. Some drug addicts deny that their drug usage affects others in an unconscious attempt to escape facing responsibility for the harm they have caused. Some cognitive-behavioral approaches simply don't confront denial on the front end of treatment, but rather lead clients through a sequential process of self-understanding in which their awareness of reality gradually and progressively increases. It is important to remember that denial exists as a way of avoiding reality — an unpleasant reality — and some counseling strategies that begin by attempting to crush a client's denial can actually create a fear and anxiety response that can cause the client to flee from treatment.

Rationalization/Justification

In the simplest of definitions, rationalizing is making justifiable excuses. Rationalization is used as a cover-up for mistakes, misjudgements, and failures. It tries to justify behavior by creating reasons that are made to sound or appear to be rational. Many treatment programs inadvertently lead clients to rationalize by asking them "why" they did certain things. In the area of relapse prevention, it is widely held that many substance abuse clients "secretly plan to relapse" by deliberately placing themselves into high risk situations where they can rationalize, "I couldn't help myself." Some clients justify their relapses by saying, "I have a progressive disease for which there is no cure." In the area of criminal rehabilitation, many offenders justify and rationalize their crimes by stating that there is no other way they can make a good living.

Projection

Projection is placing the blame for one's difficulties on others or attributing one's own unethical desires to others. Many substance abuse clients blame society, their parents, their upbringing, or others for their problems. Some clients forced into treatment angrily ask program staff "why are you doing this to me?" Projection is often seen in paranoid and suspicious patients ("everyone is talking about me or everyone is plotting against me"). In offenders, projection of their own unethical behaviors and beliefs is expressed with statements like, "Everyone else lies, cheats, and steals, why shouldn't I?"

Distortion

Distortion is a mental reshaping of a person's reality to suit inner needs. For example, many substance abusers maintain that they know more about drugs than professionals do (the abuser maintains superiority), therefore they know what they are doing with drugs and should be left alone. Some alcoholics and smokers point to family members who drank or smoked every day without having problems indicating that their genetics are superior — so they can continue to use. Some users just believe that people who become addicts are weaker than they are — "it will never happen to me." In a classic sense, distortion allows a client to feel superior and feel entitled to special treatment.

Repression

Repression is sometimes thought of as active forgetting of unpleasant thoughts or experiences. Clients in treatment will conveniently forget unpleasant experiences that occurred under the influence while tending to remember good times. It is believed that if unpleasant memories and ideas are made unconscious, then the ego can act as if the experiences never happened. Many professionals believe that most childhood sexual abuse memories are repressed, however, this remains controversial. Counselors should be aware that remembering repressed memories often precipitates a crisis that must be treated in some manner. The recall of repressed memories is not always therapeutic in and of itself and psychotherapy is a more appropriate in-depth method of attending to the therapeutic needs created by recall.

Regression

Regression is a return to an earlier, less mature developmental/ behavioral state in response to anxiety or guilt. For example, some drug addicts or alcoholics in treatment may come to the realization that they are, indeed, addicts who have created a real-life nightmare for their loved ones. In response, they might cry and even recline in the fetal position. Such experiences are not uncommon and can be used therapeutically.

Reaction Formation

Reaction formation is the prevention of dangerous behaviors/desires by actively adopting and expressing the exact opposite beliefs and behaviors. Many addicts and alcoholics become leaders in the antidrug movement or become counselors themselves. In this case, reaction formation can be a therapeutic tool. With reaction formation, however, an exaggerated opposition often appears. Statements like "you can't treat drug abuse with drugs" and "alcohol and all drugs should be outlawed" may stem from reaction formation.

Isolation/Compartmentalization

The holding of conflicting and contradictory beliefs by never thinking about them at the same time is termed isolation. The beliefs are usually thought of as being compartmentalized — tightly shut off from each other. Chemical abusers tend to have numerous areas compartmentalized. For example, some say "I love my children," yet their behavior has shown that they have done many things that indicate they don't love them. Some drug abusers state that, "I'm not a criminal," yet they have sold drugs and stolen to maintain their own habit.

Displacement

Displacement is the discharge of hostile, pent-up feelings on a person or object less dangerous than the person that initially aroused the feelings. The classic displacement example is the man who kicks his dog after his boss chews him out. In chemical abuse groups, often one person can become an object of displacement for other group members. Counselors and programs treating criminal justice clients often experience the displaced feelings of clients toward the criminal justice system that sent them there.

Fantasy

Fantasy is the gratification of frustrated desires in imaginary achievements. Some chemical abusers revel in "I could have done this or that" rather than what actually was. Fantasy, as with other defenses, isn't always pathological or bad, but it can impede a client's progress if the client sees what they "could have done" as the same thing as actually doing it.

Emotional Insulation

Emotional insulation is a withdrawal into passivity in response to anxiety or painful situations. This response can be seen in chemical dependency clients in many different circumstances. Some clients may state that, "people have been nothing but trouble to me, so from now on I'm going to just work 16 hours a day, 7 days a week, come home and eat, and go to bed." As some clients gain awareness into their difficulties, they simply become very passive or indecisive. This can occur frequently in group settings as clients gain awareness about their actions.

Undoing

Undoing is attempting to atone for or counteract negative behavior or impulses. Often compulsive behaviors, like frequent handwashing, can be attempts at undoing. In a very real sense, programs that teach clients to make amends (AA) or become a positive force in the world (MRT®) utilize undoing in a therapeutic fashion. Telling clients that they can't undo what's done, but they can atone for mistakes by changing what they do is a beneficial therapeutic tool.

Passive-Aggressive Behavior

Traditional psychoanalysis considers passive-aggressive behavior to be a form of defense mechanism. *Passive-aggression is seen when aggression toward a person or object is expressed indirectly and ineffectively through passive behavior displays, indirect gestures or behaviors, or turning against the self.* In chemical abuse treatment, passive aggressive behaviors are seen when clients are consistently late for group or sessions, when they consistently fail to complete homework or tasks required for sessions, when open, obvious gestures show their indifference or disapproval (e.g., looking out the window in group, falling asleep, yawning loudly, groaning at inappropriate times, some facial gestures) — and when they fail to openly express their hostile/indifferent attitude. Convenient forgetting, convenient sickness or accidents, and the losing of treatment materials can be passive aggressive. Many programs directly address such behaviors through confrontation and rules.

CHAPTER 3
CLIENT-CENTERED COUNSELING

If I keep from imposing on people, they become themselves.
Carl Rogers — 1972

BACKGROUND

As related in chapter 1, Client-centered counseling was first outlined by Rogers in 1938. Client-centered counseling has probably influenced the practice of counseling more than any other method. The Rogerian approach has undergone several distinct evolutionary phases.

Rogers initial development of Client-centered therapy in the 1930s and 1940s, an approach that was at variance with the prevailing views at the time, was the initial phase. In its earliest formulation, the primary role of the therapist in Client-centered counseling was to simply reflect client statements. At that time, Rogers called it "non-directive therapy" because the role of the counselor was not to steer or direct the client, but rather to assist the client to better understand themselves by restating or paraphrasing client statements. Rogers' 1951 book, *Client-Centered Therapy*, marked the second evolutionary stage of development and he began calling the approach "client-centered." The term *client* was used "to indicate that this was not a manipulative or medically prescriptive model." In his book, Rogers expanded on his views on the self and broadened the role of therapist to foster empathy — a deeper understanding of client feelings — the real or deeper meaning underlying the client's words. Results of the method on students were remarkable. In the third evolutionary phase beginning in the late 1950s, Rogers began to use and research the method on chronic schizophrenics. While the goal wasn't to "cure" schizophrenia, Rogers believed that using the technique helped both the therapist and the client better understand the inner world of the client. The fourth evolutionary period of Client-centered therapy was its transition to "person-centered therapy" beginning with Rogers' 1961 book, *On Becoming A Person*. The publication of that book led to an enormous expansion of the method into industry, business, and agency counseling. The term "person-centered" implies that rather than a client-therapist relationship, a person-to-person relationship fosters better understanding and promotes individual growth.

DEFINITION IN BRIEF

Client-centered counseling is a person-to-person therapeutic relationship between helper and client based on mutual trust, genuineness, warmth, and a deep, nonjudgemental understanding where unconditional positive regard and acceptance are prized. Careful listening, the communication of empathy and acceptance, restatement and paraphrasing, and reflection/owning of feelings are all primary methods employed. The method asserts that, by maintaining the therapeutic relationship under these key conditions, an optimal environment is created wherein clients can experience growth and self-actualization.

PHILOSOPHY/ASSUMPTIONS/ PERSONALITY THEORY

Rogers (1975) has stressed that Client-centered counseling is a philosophy, a way of life for counselors to conduct themselves. **The major assumption underlying the approach is that all individuals have a powerful and positive growth potential which has been sometimes thought of as a will to self-actualize — to reach the maximum positive potential possible.** Each person has an inherent and unique potential and, under optimal conditions, every person will self-actualize. Rogers asserted that humans are basically trusting, positive, cooperative, and rational. **The essential role of the counselor in Client-centered counseling is to provide and maintain a therapeutic relationship that creates the "optimal conditions" where clients can self-actualize.** The initial formulations of Client-centered counseling stress the maintenance of trust, warmth, acceptance of the client, and development of empathy as the basic core of the therapeutic relationship. In fact, **the *relationship* between counselor and client, in and of itself, *is* the core of Client-centered counseling.** Rogers asserts that if this relationship can be maintained and centered on the core elements (trust, acceptance, empathy, etc.), clients will self-actualize and experience growth.

Client-centered counseling does not rest upon a personality theory, but rather asserts basics about normal human growth, for example, the will to self-actualize. The approach does, however, have assumptions about what causes maladjustment. **Rogers maintains that the "denial" or "distortion" of how an individual perceives their experiences causes maladjustment.** The terms "incongruence" and "self-concept" are crucial to understanding the maladjustment processes of denial and distortion.

An individual's self concept is the sum total of how the individual values and views their experiences and internal sense of self. When a person sees their experiences in life as consistent with their thinking, feeling, and behavior, they have congruence. Incongruence occurs when a person's experiences are viewed as inconsistent or at variance with their internal self-concept. **When incongruent experiences are not incorporated in the self-concept, they are denied or distorted with maladjustment resulting.** This idea of maladjustment can easily be grasped as relevant to the treatment of alcohol and drug abusers. Many chemical abusers initially deny their problems controlling their drug use. In fact, most enter treatment with the idea and hopes of "cutting back" and gaining control over use. Their experiences with drugs or alcohol consistently show them that they can't learn to control, yet the idea that they can't use drugs at all is at variance with their self-concept. In short, there is incongruence between their experiences and their self-concept. Denial and distortion of their experiences then occur and a mass of defense mechanisms can be employed to distort and deny.

As the client becomes more aware of their own self-concept and their own experiences (through the therapeutic relationship and empathy), their self-concept incorporates the incongruent experiences resulting in congruence. As the person gains deeper insights into their actual self, the positive potentials of self-actualizing can foster beneficial changes in the person. **It is important to remember the key underlying assumptions of the method: it assumes rationality and a positive will (a force or striving) for each person to self-actualize.**

TERMINOLOGY &
ESSENTIAL KEY CONCEPTS

Actualizing Tendency —

A reliable and inherent predisposition in humans to grow to their maximum potentials under free and optimal conditions. The actualizing tendency can be hindered or stopped by certain environmental and psychological conditions.

Empathy/Empathic Attitudes —

An accurate and sensitive understanding of the feelings and experiences of others; considered to be a crucial characteristic of therapists to enter the client's world and "feel at home" there. It is a here-and-now understanding of the client's inner world that can also foster greater understanding of the client to both helper and client.

Experiencing —

Everything that is occurring within the person that is available to the person's awareness. Some experiences are not quite to the level of awareness and are unclearly "felt" or vaguely understood. As experiences move to full awareness they are "felt" fully in the moment; this process is aided by empathy and is considered to be an important part of the therapeutic process.

Genuineness/Congruence —

Considered to be the basic attitudes of a Client-centered helper and is expressed by the helper being "for real." The therapist is "transparent" when genuine in that the inner, real self is the same as the outer, perceived self. Congruence is when the experiences of the "outer self" coincide with, and are incorporated into, the self-concept.

Incongruence —

When some behavior, feelings, or thoughts are not in accordance with the self-concept or incorporated into the self-concept. Incongruence leads to a blocking of actualization.

Self/Self-Concept —

The total thoughts, feelings, behavior, and experiences that a person identifies as the "me" of the personality. It includes the relationships of "me" to the outside world and the relative value or importance of everything to the person. Self-concept is the internal "entity" of a person.

Unconditional Positive Regard (Caring) —

An attitude displayed by the helper that conveys a genuine caring for the client demonstrating unconditional, nonjudgemental warmth in which the client is accepted fully as he or she is in the present. This attitude fosters trust, self-exploration, and empathy.

COUNSELING PROCESS — In Brief

Rogers has described the Client-centered process as one in which the client models or reciprocates the attitudes and behaviors of the helper. Thus, a helper who begins by trying to understand the client's experiences and experiencing process fosters client empathy by showing empathy. The counselor's primary goal is one of understanding the client while maintaining attitudes and behavior that foster deeper sharing and understanding. The helper shows care and warmth, truly being genuine and transparent by showing the client that the helper cares for, understands, and prizes the client as he or she is right now. Client feelings, statements, gestures and other nonverbal behavior are attended to and reflected back to the client in paraphrases, feelings reflection, and in a sharing of the helper's own responses to the client. During the entire process, the helper maintains an attitude of unconditional positive regard without judgement, suspicion, or defensiveness. Unconditional acceptance of the client's joyful and painful experiences is sought. There are times in the beginning of the therapeutic process that the helper inquires, "how are you feeling right now?" The reflections of the client's feelings can lead to a deeper level of understanding and foster trust.

As the therapeutic relationship deepens and the client develops a real sense of trust, the client will tend to explore the self at deeper levels. In a very real sense, the client becomes increasingly free to express deeper feelings, deeper personal meanings, and significant experiences that are incongruent with the client's self-concept. Ownership of feelings, a focus on self (as opposed to nonself issues), and in increase in self-awareness result.

With increasing awareness, the client begins to fully experience incongruences and discrepancies in behavior and self. As this process occurs, the client assimilates such awareness into their self-concept and becomes more congruent. Rogers has defined the process of becoming more congruent as a process of psychological adjustment which lowers a client's resistance to change. In short, the client begins to feel less threatened by internal and external processes and begins to better understand self and their relationship to the outer world.

A fundamental underpinning is the client's will to self-actualize. As clients become more congruent, they have less to defend and distort and they become increasingly effective in coping with problems of all kinds — tensions decrease, experiences are seen as positive and constructive, and confidence in self-determination become apparent. Since the client can now understand and differentiate between satisfactory and unsatisfactory experiences, he or she is better able to make choices that lead to satisfactory outcomes.

It is important to understand that Rogers assumes that clients are essentially positive and rational but that when distortion and denial occur, certain maladjustments occur. By maintaining an optimal growth environment in the therapeutic relationship, counselors can allow clients to make positive and beneficial changes that will lead to self-actualization.

APPROPRIATE USE/LIMITS

Rogers essentially placed no limits on his counseling approach. He has asserted that listening to clients, unconditional caring for them, and understanding lead to beneficial changes, however, research on substance abusers, psychotics, and other diagnoses has indicated clear limits on the method's ability to effectively reduce presenting symptoms in some clients. While Client-centered therapists have "worked with" schizophrenics, the mentally retarded, devepopmentally disabled, and virtually all other diagnoses, many professionals consider the method ineffective with some clients.

Limits of Client-centered therapy sometimes relate to the possibility of client manipulation of the counselor and ineffectiveness on the client's presenting symptoms. Gilliland, James, and Bowman (1994) state that many counselors appear to think they understand and use the method, but in reality they misunderstand and misuse it. The method is not as easy to implement as it may appear. Maintenance of unconditional positive regard and unwavering trust may be difficult — if not impractical — with certain clients. For example, substance abusers from criminal justice almost always have problems with "trust" (many such clients have a lot to "hide"). Clients that are the best candidates for the approach are described as having contact with reality, average or above intellectual abilities, and average or above communication skills.

Gilliland, et. al. (1994) have provided an excellent summary of situations and clients that are appropriate for Client-centered therapy. When therapists are counseling clients from different cultural backgrounds, the approach is often helpful — especially in the beginning of the therapeutic relationship. Clients experiencing loneliness, dealing with grief (a death or loss of a special relationship), encountering problems with aging (gerontological counseling), and dealing with disabilities are especially appropriate. In addition, Client-centered therapy remains perhaps the best approach for guidance counseling applications where students and others making vocational and educational decisions are counseled to assist with the decision. Rogers especially focused on the use of Client-centered counseling in groups.

In regards to substance abuse counseling, Client-centered counseling is not appropriate as the only approach used with criminal justice clients. Even Gilliland, et. al. cite that the use of the approach with clients that need structured guidance, reinforcement, and concrete goals is often inappropriate. It is possible — and often desirable — in some types of chemical abuse treatment programs for counselors to perform the approach in individual and group counseling sessions. In such programs the use of the method may be quite useful in establishing a therapeutic relationship with clients.

Despite these reservations, the essentials of Client-centered therapy remain the cornerstones of substance abuse counseling and are required knowledge for counselors facing state and national certification/licensure tests. Thus, it is recommended that substance abuse counselors develop both the basic skills and knowledge in the method.

CHAPTER 4
BEHAVIORISM

Three major approaches to psychotherapy dominate contemporary
clinical psychology: psychoanalysis, behavior modification, and
the phenomenological therapies.
Goldenberg — (1973) *Contemporary Clinical Psychology*

BACKGROUND

Although it might not be readily apparent, most chemical
dependency counselors and programs extensively utilize behavioral
techniques. Programs analyze client symptoms, reinforce desired
behaviors, punish unwanted behaviors, and employ relapse prevention, relaxation training, assertion training, modeling, role playing,
and various other purely behavioral methods. Therapeutic communities and many residential programs use peer hierarchies where
advanced clients serve as role models for newer clients. Clients
progress through the peer hierarchy by displaying appropriate
behavior and receive increased privileges and rewards as they move
up in the hierarchy. In short, behaviorism has greatly influenced the
systematic process of chemical abuse counseling. Behavioral counseling techniques represent a broad range of strategies and should
not be thought of as a single system of helping (Gilliland, et. al., 1990).
Behavioral techniques rest upon a foundation of scientific learning
theory that asserts much of human behavior is learned and can be
unlearned.

Behavioral treatment strategies historically are traced to the
American psychologist Edward Thorndike (1898) and Bekhterev
(1912) and Pavlov (1927) in the former Soviet Union. These early
researchers demonstrated that much animal behavior is learned with
two primary types of learning processes demonstrated. Pavlov's
research showed the existence of the first: what is today known as
classical conditioning — or *respondent conditioning*. Pavlov showed that

dogs could be trained to reflexively salivate to the sound of a bell if the dogs had first been exposed to the simultaneous presentation of the bell with food. *Behavior therapy* has developed treatment methods from these findings. In 1920, John Watson and Rosalie Rayner showed how some human fears could be conditioned (learned) by the same process. An 11-month-old infant named "Albert" was exposed to a small white laboratory rat that the baby reached out to touch. At the moment the baby touched the rat, the experimenters created a loud sound by striking a steel bar with a hammer. Babies are reflexively frightened of loud sounds, so the infant cried and withdrew his hand. The researchers then paired the loud sound with only the visual presentation of the rat for five trials. The baby began to cry when the rat was in view. Four months later, the child still cried at the sight of the rat. In addition, the child became afraid of other small white objects including rabbits, dogs, and even a fur coat. This process is termed *generalization*. This classic study has shown how some emotions might be conditioned or learned and can spread or generalize to other similar stimuli. Various researchers also demonstrated how such conditioning could be reversed (unlearned). Jones (1924), a student of Watson, showed how fear of furry animals could be first learned and then unlearned through systematic methods. Wolpe (1958) formally introduced the process of *systematic desensitization* demonstrating how many fears, phobias, and anxiety-provoking situations could be successfully treated through learning principles.

Classical conditioning examples are observed in substance abusers and addressed in relapse prevention treatment. For example, Myers (1992) cites the cravings that former crack users will feel when they are exposed to their usual drug-using environment. In relapse prevention, the "drug using environment" is appropriately seen as a high-risk situation because the use of drugs has been repeatedly paired with being in that particular environment. Thus, drug users feel cravings when exposed to the people, places, and things associated with drug usage because repeated pairings have produced conditioning. Aversive counterconditioning is also frequently cited as a method employed with alcoholics. For example, when a drug that causes nausea and vomiting is mixed into an alcohol drink and then consumed by an alcoholic, the aversive feelings following the alcohol consumption are conditioned to the use of alcohol. Repeated trials of this pairing (alcohol consumption + nausea/vomiting) are required for aversive conditioning. In addition, some aversive conditioning studies have paired alcohol consumption with electrical shocks. Some results have shown that a reduction of alcohol consumption does occur under these laboratory conditions, but "booster shot trials" are often required. Individual differences in alcohol reactivity and researchers' inability to control for alcohol use outside the laboratory setting have produced inconsistent results with these procedures (Franks, 1963; Morosco & Baer, 1970; Wiens & Menustik, 1983). From a historical and purist viewpoint, *behavior therapy* is the term used to identify treatment procedures derived from classical/ respondent conditioning.

It should be noted that aversive conditioning for alcohol/ drug use is controversial. Such procedures usually are controlled laboratory experiments and counselors are unlikely to be involved with these experiments. It is, however, important that substance abuse counselors have some familiarity with the research cited.

The second primary learning early researchers identified is called operant conditioning. Historically, treatment methods derived from operant conditioning have traditionally been referred to as *behavior management.* The term "operant" is derived from the observation that animals and humans operate or manipulate their environment with behavior to obtain rewards or avoid aversive stimuli. Burrhus F. Skinner is the best known theorist of operant conditioning. Skinner's research initially began to investigate the various parameters of Throndike's *law of effect:* the fact that *rewarded behavior is likely to recur*. Skinner found that various schedules of reinforcement predictably resulted in behavior. From this simple position, drug usage is reinforced, therefore it tends to recur. The fact that drug usage is so hard to extinguish as a behavior stems from the immediacy of the reward, the varying schedules of partial reinforcement encountered with drug use, and the association of other positive reinforcers with drug use (people, places, things). A number of useful methodologies have emerged from operant conditioning concepts. Bandura's (1969) concept of *social learning* or *modeling*, the learning of new behaviors by imitating others' behavior, is extensively employed in drug treatment programs. Modeling, or observational learning, is an important component of an individual learning *prosocial skills* — behaviors leading to positive, helpful results with others. In recent years, substance abusing offenders have been found to have deficits in various social skills and many programs are required to teach prosocial skills that directly address these deficits. In addition, a large number of programs utilize a token economy or some variation of it. Points, tokens or chips, or some other measurable item are awarded to program clients for positive, desirable behavior. As clients accumulate points or tokens, they can earn other privileges or rewards. Programs often term such systems as phase or level systems or simply refer to it as a peer hierarchy. In addition, behavioral contracting, identifying target behaviors (both desirable and undesirable), goal setting, establishing rewards, and self-management are behavior management techniques. Finally, controlled drinking methods (attempts to teach drinkers to control their consumption) are also a form of behavioral management. While extremely controversial, to say the least, it is doubtful if controlled drinking strategies produce any long-term beneficial changes in alcoholics.

Starting in the mid-1980s, behavioral practitioners began merging ideas and techniques with cognitive theory resulting in cognitive-behavioral therapy. Cognitive-behavioral therapy is one of the most important current methodologies used with substance abusers. A large and varying number of cognitive-behavioral techniques exist today. Cognitive-behavioral therapy has become so important that it considered to be a separate counseling approach, therefore, it will be covered separately in a later chapter.

DEFINITION IN BRIEF

Behavioral counseling represents a systematic application of learning principles and techniques to the treatment of behavioral disorders utilizing a wide-range of procedures. The method includes *behavior therapy* techniques (systematic desensitization, relaxation training, assertion training, aversion therapies) and *behavior management* techniques (social learning/modeling, role-playing, token economies, reward systems used with patients in programs, behavioral contracting). Cognitive-behavioral strategies represent a recent outgrowth of a merging of behavior theory with cognitive theory and are considered to be a separate counseling theory.

PHILOSOPHY/ASSUMPTIONS/ PERSONALITY THEORY

A major tenant of behaviorism is *personality is learned.* Thus, pathological or maladjustive behavior is learned. A common example used to explain this is shyness. Shyness is often learned early in life through a series of events. For example, the shy individual may have been frequently ignored or scolded for assertive behavior. (Being ignored can extinguish behavior as it often represents lack of reinforcement; being scolded usually represents punishment and tends to result in the suppression of behavior.) At other times, the individual may have been rewarded (or not punished) for staying quiet, remaining out of sight, and keeping their thoughts private. Over time, the individual found that the behaviors described as shy produced reward and/or avoided punishment. In situations where the individual became the center of attention, anxiety and tension emerged (a learned response that seems to anticipate a punishment). As the person avoided being the center of attention, their anxiety dissipated thus reinforcing the behavior of shyness. (Behavior that results in less anxiety tends to be repeated.) In short, once established, shy behaviors become part of a self-reinforcing system.

Drug using behavior is learned from the behavioral perspective. Drugs that are not found to be rewarding to the individual are not used again. Drugs that produce reward — or reinforcement (e.g., they feel good) — are used over and over. Because of certain biological or genetic differences, some individuals find the use of some drugs more appealing or rewarding than others. The concept that drug users have a preferred "drug of choice" may reflect this behavioral philosophy. In addition, some drug use is maintained by the rewards of being around particular people, places, or situations that the user finds rewarding. Social rewards, generalization of drug usage to many other situations, and respondent conditioning are all part of drug usage. Psychologists frequently cite the fact that animals, provided the opportunity, will use and become dependent on the same drugs as humans — showing that drug use is inherently reinforcing to behavior rather than some deeper personality issues causing the drug usage (see the text *Psychopharmacology* [Little, 1997] for a review of the "addictive personality" versus reinforcement controversy of drug usage).

Behavioral counseling maintains a focus on observable behaviors. Other than establishing the conditions under which behaviors are performed and the consequences of the behavior, behaviorists do not give much concern to the etiology or causes of problems. Behaviorists believe that anxiety, nervousness, tension, fear, anger, guilt, depression, and many physical conditions (e.g., some headaches, upset stomach) stem from conditioning — learned responses to events or the anticipation of these events. The focus of behavioral techniques is to assist clients to "unlearn" these maladaptive behaviors and have clients establish new, alternate, and appropriate behaviors.

Behaviorists recognize that all organisms have biological predispositions (Myers, 1992) and that even when conditioning has established new behavioral patterns, organisms tend to revert to their "old ways." "Booster shots" of reconditioning are sometimes employed to maintain desired behaviors. In summary, behaviorists focus on observable behaviors, target desired changes in the behavior, manipulate the environment to extinguish undesired behavior while reinforcing desired behavior, and seek to maintain desired changes.

TERMINOLOGY & ESSENTIAL KEY CONCEPTS

Substance abuse counselors who choose to include behavioral counseling as one of their three counseling theories should be familiar with a variety of terms and techniques. Some counselors who serve on verbal exam boards occasionally assert that cognitive-behavioral counseling is a type of behavioral counseling. Thus, it would be wise for counselors taking exams to be able to clearly and succinctly differentiate between methods and terms. Behavioral techniques typically have precise definitions and the following list will provide a working knowledge of these terms. The following definitions are a composite from Chapin (1975), Goldenberg (1973), Wolman (1973), and others.

Schedules of Reinforcement —
A schedule of reinforcement is the frequency at which reinforcement is delivered following a behavior or response. For example, when a reinforcement is delivered each time a behavior is performed, the schedule is *continuous*. Most human behavior is reinforced with

a *partial reinforcement* schedule. For example, a fisherman doesn't usually catch a fish each time he or she casts. Partial reinforcement schedules are very difficult to extinguish (the behaviors are persistent). Several types of partial reinforcement schedules exist based upon time and the amount of behavior necessary to get the reinforcement. *Fixed-ratio* schedules deliver reinforcement after a set number of behavioral responses. Some fruit pickers are paid by the bushel — thus, their reinforcement is set by how many bushels they can pick. *Variable-ratio* schedules reinforce behavior with a variable number of responses but based on an average. When casinos advertise that they have a 91% pay-back on slot machines, what they are saying is that as people sit pumping quarters into the machines in the casino, that all the gamblers will "win" an average of 91% of the money put into the machines. In short, the slots will frequently reward players, but it takes a lot of quarters for the rewards — the casino has preset all the slot machines to pay 91% of the money back to "winners" on a variable schedule. Behaviors reinforced by variable-ratio schedules are very difficult to extinguish — a simple fact that can be observed at casinos. *Fixed-interval* schedules deliver the reinforcement after a set time. For example, a paycheck each Friday is set on a fixed interval. *Variable-interval* schedules reward a behavior after a varying, unpredictable time period. This schedule produces a steady rate of behavior. Drug usage behavior is not reinforced by continuous reinforcement schedules. First, it's important to understand that the effects of the drug on the user represent only one possible reward or reinforcement. Other reinforcers include activities with certain people who are associated with drug usage, avoidance of aversive activities, and association with drug usage with other rewarding activities (like music, food, parties). Drug usage is reinforced by almost all of the partial reinforcement schedules. Thus, it is a very, very difficult behavior to extinguish.

Reinforcement —

A consequence of a behavior that increases the chances that the behavior will be repeated. Feeling good after taking a drug is experienced as rewarding and thus reinforces drug taking behavior. This is an example of *positive reinforcement. Negative reinforcers* increase behavior by removing or reducing an aversive or unpleasant condition. For example, if a person is feeling depressed (an aversive, unpleasant condition) finds that cocaine relieves the depression, the drug taking behavior is reinforced by the relief of the aversive condition.

Punishment —

A consequence of behavior that decreases the chances that a behavior will be performed. Punishment is usually the withdrawal of positive reinforcers (like removing privileges and favored activities like TV) or, more often, the delivery of an aversive condition (like a spanking or jail time). Punishment can "suppress" behavior temporarily, the punished person often performs the undesired behavior out of the presence of the punisher. It may foster aggression or learned helplessness and create fear.

Behavioral Shaping —

A process of guiding behavior toward some final, desired response through the systematic delivery of reinforcement. *Successive approximation*, the delivery of reinforcement as behavior moves closer and closer to the desired response, is a form of behavioral shaping.

Behavioral Assessment/Analysis —

A fundamental starting point for much behavioral counseling where overt behavior is analyzed and targeted for change. Defining maladaptive behavior, measuring a baseline of frequency, determining environmental conditions and reinforcers, and planning for alterations in the environment are all part of the process.

Systematic Desensitization/Reciprocal Inhibition —

An important technique designed by Wolpe (1958) to countercondition fear/anxiety producing stimuli. The method often begins with the patient developing a hierarchy of anxiety producing situations; learning relaxation techniques; systematically pairing the anxiety-producing images with deep relaxation. Reciprocal inhibition is a term that describes the intent of the procedure: it is not possible to be relaxed and anxious at the same time.

Aversive Counterconditioning —

The replacement of a positive reinforcer (e.g., feeling good) with an aversive consequence (e.g., feeling sick) for a particular behavior. The method is used with smokers, alcoholics, and some other drug users.

Modeling/Role Playing —

Modeling is also called observational learning — watching others and imitating behavior. Role playing is a way to understand and practice a role by acting "as if" in a contrived situation.

Token Economies —

The systematic use of reinforcers and sometimes punishment in the context of a treatment environment. In the classic token economy, clients have some choice in the rewards that their accumulated tokens or "points" can acquire.

Assertion Training —

A method devised by Wolpe to teach inhibited clients overt behaviors that are the exact opposite of inhibition. Modern usages teach clients to stand up for their rights, negotiate firmly and fairly, be less aggressive and respectful while remaining assertive, and express their feelings and desires.

Self-Management/Contracting

A technique wherein a client enters into a time-based contract with the counselor or others to reach desired goals. The contract stipulates precisely what the desired goals are, how and when they are measured, what the reinforcements or punishments may be, and how and when the consequences for behaviors are delivered.

COUNSELING PROCESS — In Brief

The behavioral counseling process begins by listening and communicating with the patient to identify problem behaviors. Trust, warmth, and empathy, while usually considered to be a desirable trait of counselors, are not always essential in behavioral approaches. (Note that trust and warmth do foster patient cooperation in the treatment process and are very helpful with all types of clients. Behavioral counselors should seek to develop and maintain these conditions, however, the philosophy of the approach does not dictate them.) In some cases, the client assists the behavioral counselor with identifying problem behaviors and setting goals. In other cases (e.g., criminal justice supervision clients) the counselor may have goals that are essentially dictated to the client. The desired behaviors, consequences of behaviors (both desired and undesired) are defined and outlined to the client (sometimes with the client's consent and agreement), types of appropriate conditioning methods are defined (e.g., relaxation training, role-playing groups), and time frames are addressed. The plan is then followed, but changes and adaptations will be made based upon the client's unique needs or environmental circumstances.

It is essential that counselors be precise and nonbiased, follow through with consequences, carefully observe client behavior, and respond according to client behavior rather than counselor "feelings/intuitions." In reality, many counselors employ behavioral methods within a program's operating procedures, but also perform individual counseling from some other orientation. It is important that clients not get mixed messages from staff. For example, a program may have punished a client for drug usage (a dirty urine screen) by having the client leave urine screens for 7 consecutive days. The counselor who sees the client individually should refrain from discussions about how the punishment is unfair. The counselor could explore the client's feelings regarding the unfairness or inconvenience of the punishment, but caution should be taken by the counselor to not tell the client that the counselor agrees that the punishment is unfair.

Modern behavioral practitioners tend to be friendly, caring, and trusting counselors and this attitude usually fosters better client cooperation and appropriate behavioral change. Behavioral counseling, however, focuses on altering overt behavior — not exploring the past for causes, trying to foster insight, or deeply exploring client feelings. The method can be employed in group settings with role playing, modeling, discussions on behavior and outcomes of behavior, defining reinforcers and punishments, discussing clients' progress on targeted goals, and in structured behavioral exercises.

APPROPRIATE USE/LIMITS

Behavioral methods are most appropriate when the important issues in treatment are specific, measurable outcomes. Chemical abuse treatment is one of the most noticeable areas where behaviorism has had a significant, measurable impact. In particular, the use of behavioral group and individual counseling techniques lead to significant reductions in drug/alcohol offenders' recidivism (Andrews, 1994; Gendreau, 1995; Little & Robinson, 1997; Palmer, 1993). Meta-analyses of offender treatment data show that the reduction of recidivism attributed to behavioral programming range from 8% to 25%. Therapeutic communities appear to produce recidivism reductions in the same range.

Behavioral methods are also appropriate with specific problems such as fears, anxiety, shyness, aggressive problems, sexual problems, parenting, and vocational problems. Critics of behaviorism point to the fact that only the client's presenting problem is the focus of behavioral treatment — not the cause, client feelings, development of insight, or history. Critics also state that a "symptom substitution" occurs (when one symptom goes away, another emerges). However, outcome data has not supported this basic contention. Some critics like to point out Skinner's contention that organisms actually have no freedom and that behavioral techniques restrict the freedom of clients.

Behaviorism is probably least effective — and can sometimes be considered inappropriate — for normal grief after a loss, some elderly issues, when clients first face debilitating conditions, and at the beginning of a therapeutic relationship with clients of vastly differing cultures.

CHAPTER 5
RATIONAL-EMOTIVE THERAPY

RET represents one of the most radical and directive
approaches in modern psychotherapy.
Strupp & Blackwood — (1975)

BACKGROUND

Rational-Emotive Therapy (RET) was developed by Albert
Ellis in the mid-1950s and is considered to be the forerunner of
modern cognitive-behavioral therapies (CBT). Some professionals
consider the "general" application of RET to be synonymous with
CBT. RET is sometimes termed rational therapy, rational behavior
therapy, and semantic therapy (Gilliland, et. al., 1994). The direct
application of RET to chemical abusers has been presented in the text,
Rational-Emotive Therapy With Alcoholics and Substance Abusers (Ellis,
McInerney, DiGiuseppe, & Yeager, 1988). Those interested should
refer to that text for a more in-depth explanation of the method
applied to chemical abusers.

Ellis, a psychoanalytically-trained psychologist, was frustrated by the poor outcomes of slow, tedious, and non-directive
traditional therapy. Ellis began to understand that clients' problems
stemmed from neither external events in their lives nor from their
past, but rather from how they perceived or interpreted events. Thus,
client beliefs or cognitions formed the basis of their core problems.
RET is a method that directly confronts irrational beliefs and behavior
in an effort to have clients abandon them (Strupp & Blackwood,
1975).

Regarding the treatment of alcoholics, Ellis has written that
he found other methods unsuccessful during 1943 to 1953 when he
was using traditional approaches and uncovering unresolved
childhood trauma (Ellis, 1991). In addition, Ellis found the AA
concept of "Higher Power" and an admission of total lack of control

to be irrational and antitherapeutic. After employing the RET concepts on alcoholics, Ellis found a much higher success rate. An RET based alternative to AA, called Rational Recovery was developed in 1985 by an RET trained social worker Jack Trimpey. Training in RET is provided today by Ellis' New York-based Institute for Rational-Emotive Therapy.

DEFINITION IN BRIEF

RET was the first form of cognitive-behavior therapy and emphasizes a philosophic and active, directive approach to prevention and treatment of disorders. It utilizes both emotive-evocative techniques (like direct confrontation of beliefs and behavior) and behavior therapy (e.g., homework). The method teaches that an individual's beliefs about events determine both emotional and behavioral responses. Irrational beliefs about self and the world lead to irrational, self-defeating behavior. RET helps clients identify irrational beliefs and behavior and replace them with rationality.

PHILOSOPHY/ASSUMPTIONS/ PERSONALITY THEORY

RET asserts that human behavior is greatly influenced by biological predispositions. In the mid-1970s, Ellis wrote that only 20% or so of all human behavior is determined by environment or learning with the rest determined by biological predispositions. CBT practitioners also address and acknowledge the biological basis of behavior, however, modern research in genetics and behavioral genetics have found that genetic programming greatly influences some disorders while other disorders are influenced by biology to a much smaller degree. For example, Cluster-B personality disorders (e.g., Antisocial Personality Disorder) is believed to be 30%-50% genetic while the genetic predisposition to alcoholism or drug addiction is much less — 10%-30% (see *Psychopharmacology* [Little, 1997] for a review). The relevance of the biological predisposition to treatment is that biology can't be altered, but a client's beliefs and behavior can be changed — their philosophy about life can change. Thus, the beliefs and cognitions should be the focus of treatment rather than uncovering the early childhood trauma or environmental events that many professionals assume cause the disorder.

Starting from the assumption that much of what makes an individual unique stems from biological predispositions, the remainder of personality forms from beliefs that an individual *teaches* him- or herself. Ellis believes that humans have an inherent tendency to "want and to insist that everything happens for the best in their life" (Ellis, 1979). When things don't happen the way people want, they irrationally condemn others, the world, or themselves — thereby producing irrational emotions and behavior that lead to maladjustment and problems. Related to this idea is that people who have *low frustration tolerance* — an inability to "put up with" not immediately getting what they want — develop problems of anxiety, depression, procrastination, agoraphobia, or giving up without effort. Low frustration tolerance is based upon a foundation of irrational beliefs. Drug and alcohol use both yield short-term, immediate gratification from a hedonistic (pleasure seeking / pain avoidance) viewpoint. Thus, the use of drugs and alcohol can lead to behaviors that are gratifying in the short-term, but destructive in the long-term. Low frustration tolerance leads to relapse, avoidance of responsibility, blaming, and self-condemnation — all of which are irrational from the RET viewpoint.

Countering the underlying irrationality of humans is a strong tendency for humans to also grow in a positive sense toward self-actualization. Thus, RET rests upon a humanistic foundation that has similarities to other humanistic systems and Adlerian concepts. Actualizing in RET is sometimes defined as maximizing happiness over the long-term through social contexts. It is assumed that once an individual learns to identify and alter irrational beliefs and behavior, that more rational beliefs and behavior replace them. It is the role of the therapist to foster client identification of irrational beliefs and teach more rational ideas and behaviors. Thus, in RET, the therapist serves as an educator, coach, expert, and scientist.

Research has indicated that all people of all cultures, regardless of intelligence, background, education, or social standing have irrational beliefs and behavior. The degree of an individual's emotional / behavioral problems are a direct result of the degree of irrational thinking and irrational behavior a particular person has. Individuals *teach* themselves irrational beliefs by self-indoctrination using repetitive phrases and sentences that serve a self-reinforcing, circular, and sometimes self-defeating purpose. For example, a person may engage in repeatedly thinking, "I can't do math." This continual self-talk creates *low frustration tolerance* (the individual is likely to give up without much effort) and become a *self-fulfilling prophecy* at test time. Confronting irrational "self-talk" is a role of the RET practitioner. Such self-talk is prevalent in chemical abusers. Many abusers repeatedly say to themselves, "I can't stop using."

Ellis categorizes irrational beliefs (beliefs are not facts but rather ideas we accept as truth) into several categories. One type of irrational belief is *demandingness* of self, others, and the world. Demands are stated as absolutes and often have the words "should, must, ought, have to" in them: "You *must* treat me fairly. I *must* get this job. You *should* allow me another chance. The world *ought* to be fair. I *have to* go out with this person." RET teaches clients to understand that such demands are actually wants and preferences rather than absolute requirements for happiness. Another type of irrational belief is *awfulizing* which occurs when a person evaluates a situation as worse than it is. For example, a client might state: "Being in drug treatment is *awful*." The client is sometimes asked by the RET practitioner, "is this the *worst* thing that could *possibly* happen? It may be unfortunate and create temporary anxiety, but it isn't as awful as a lot of other alternatives." The method referred to as *cognitive restructuring* frequently utilizes this procedure.

Many irrational beliefs stem from perceptions of self and others. For example, many offenders state that, "the system is totally unfair." RET practitioners may dispute this irrational belief by asking, "can you think of anyone who got locked up and actually deserved it?" Clients may also state, "I'm a weak person, so I take drugs or drink." RET practitioners may have the person think of something that they did that showed strength or control over behavior and reply — "You can be strong when you want to."

Another category of irrational beliefs concern beliefs about the future. In particular, overgeneralizations about possible future outcomes (e.g., "I'll never overcome this problem") can set up self-fulfilling prophecies.

RET teaches clients practical solutions to change things in their life that they can by utilizing problem solving, decision making skills, and communication. RET also teaches clients to change their view of unchangeable events in their lives to a more rational, accepting one. Central to this approach is the ABC method (described on the next page).

TERMINOLOGY &
ESSENTIAL KEY CONCEPTS

ABC Theory —
  In analyzing client behavior, the sequence of events is broken down into an understandable ABC sequence. A represents an *Activating Event* — usually an external life event that seems to provoke our behavioral response. For example, if a client was laid off from his job, that event could be seen as an Activating Event. In response, the client could say that he got depressed and drank. This behavior represents a *consequence* - **C**. At first glance, many people would say that the **A** (job loss) caused **C** (the drinking). But between **A** and **C** is **B** — the client's *beliefs*. Irrational beliefs can cause maladaptive behavior. The client could think, "Losing my job is awful, I can't stand this" or "I'm such a total failure." Other examples would be, "this shouldn't happen to me" or "They treated me totally unfairly." Emotional reactions are attached to beliefs such that some clients could think, "how totally unfair. Here I am trying to make it and now this happens. This is just awful, I feel terrible, so I'll go relieve the stress with a drink." A major portion of RET sessions is consumed by identifying the ABCs, especially the beliefs.

Activating Events —
  As related above, activating events are usually external events that seem to provoke responses. Ellis stresses that we live in a world with countless stresses and difficult life situations. Learning to control and change activating events that are within our control is a part of RET as is identifying activating events outside of our control. Such noncontrollable events can be accepted philosophically as a part of life. It is our interpretation of activating events that is a key.

Irrational Beliefs —
  Irrational beliefs typically cause inappropriate emotions and behavior. Irrational beliefs are ideas that are contradicted by facts or reality. Irrational beliefs are usually stated as absolutes, are inconsistent and illogical, lead to unhappiness or feelings of misery, and produce blaming of others and the world for personal problems.

Musturbation —

A form of self-talk (beliefs that are repetitively thought or verbalized) where a person makes irrational demands or commands about self or others. Musturbation occurs when a person comes to see their preferences and wants in life as necessities. For example, the belief that "I must, ought, should, have to have the love and admiration of others" leads to three irrational beliefs: *awfulizing* about things, *self-damnation*, and what Ellis terms *"I-can't-stand-it-itis."*

Low Frustration Tolerance —

The inability to put up with short-term discomfort for long-term rewards is low frustration tolerance. People who demand that the world deliver to them everything they want when they want it, the idea that when we don't get what we want that the world is unfair and unjust and it's terrible, and that such situations are awful (I-can't-stand-it-itis) are consequences of low frustration tolerance.

Locus of Control —

Internal locus of control is associated with the belief that the individual creates his or her reality — that the individual controls their behavior and emotions. External locus of control is seen when people blame others for their problems and difficulties, when they attribute their failures to bad luck, and when they feel helpless.

Rational Thinking —

Comprised of several characteristic elements including: beliefs derived from objective facts, the behavior stemming from the belief is self-protective, helps the individual define appropriate personal goals, produces a minimum of conflict with self and others.

Parables —

Used in RET to assist clients to understand ideas and beliefs that may not be fully understood. For example, the author has found the saying, *wickedness, like misery, loves company*, useful with substance abusers. Clients are asked to define what they think the saying means.

Paradoxical Intention —

A specific method designed to allow clients to understand

the irrationality of a behavior or belief by encouraging the client to practice or rehearse the irrational act. The method is similar to what is called the "Midas technique" and is related to another RET method called reduction to absurdity — taking a client's belief to its extremes.

Disputing Irrational Beliefs —

A central method of RET employing many techniques and procedures. One method is to find the exception to a client's statement to show the belief isn't completely true. For example, if a client says, I drink because I'm depressed," a useful question might be, "have you ever drank at a time you weren't depressed?"

Homework —

RET utilizes homework in a very active manner making assignments for clients to face fears, practice positive behaviors, and identify irrational beliefs.

COUNSELING PROCESS — In Brief

Ellis, et. al. (1988) have outlined the RET process for substance abusers. It is stressed that the relationship between therapist and client is interpersonal, but that specific qualities (like a warm, caring therapist attitude) are not sufficient or necessary for appropriate client changes. Ellis does, however, stress that if the client feels an alliance with the therapist, that the client will be more willing to undertake therapy. In RET, the therapist develops a trusting relationship and accepts the client while building client confidence in the therapist's ability. RET practitioners take on a scientific, expert-like role, thus, it is important that therapists be accurate in information as well as able to confront irrationality.

Initial sessions establish a collaborative relationship where the therapist listens and attends to client statements, asks appropriate questions, and occasionally teaches. It is essential to avoid generalizations like, "all addicts want to continue to use drugs." Even in the initial session, RET practitioners identify and target key problem areas. Key irrational beliefs in clients are often evident early in therapy.

Homework is often assigned in early sessions like listening to specific self-help tapes or reading specific brochures. This seeks to have the client quickly understand that a large part of the RET process is self-help. Assessments take place in early sessions and continue throughout therapy. These are designed to uncover self-defeating beliefs and behavior. RET practitioners form and test hypotheses about clients routinely often with a version of the question: "What do you need help with now?" Realistic treatment goals and client behavior goals are collaboratively set and assessed each session.

Throughout each RET session, client statements and beliefs are challenged, disputed, and put to the test. The ABC method of assessing problematic situations and responses is frequently employed. The RET therapist employs numerous techniques as appropriate in sessions as the client's behavior is encouraged to become more rational and productive.

In general, it is assumed that as irrational beliefs change to rational beliefs, that both appropriate philosophical and behavioral changes occur at the same time. Sessions often begin by obtaining a report by the client on homework assignments, problems encountered since the last session, and reviewing the treatment goals. Challenging and disputing irrational beliefs — utilizing any of the various means — is a continual process.

APPROPRIATE USE/LIMITS

RET is certainly useful and appropriate for chemical abuse clients, shyness, lack of assertive behavior, phobias, and a variety of other problems (Strupp & Blackwood, 1975). Others have cited the finding that some clients expect a therapist to be an expert and an authority and RET is especially useful with such clients (Young, 1986). Ellis has stated that RET is not appropriate for children, active psychotics, and the mentally handicapped. Critics of RET cite the de-emphasis of the therapist-client relationship, the fact that RET doesn't let clients "work through feelings," and the possibility that there is a risk of client harm. (This risk has never been substantiated by outcome data.) Finally, and perhaps most importantly, many counselors find it difficult to identify and challenge irrational beliefs. Some inexperienced chemical abuse counselors are prone to make sweeping generalizations about drugs and client characteristics — many of which are not borne out by facts. In general, counselors with higher educations and more training find RET useful and manageable as a counseling method.

CHAPTER 6
REALITY THERAPY

"...therapy is a special kind of teaching or training which attempts
to accomplish in a relatively short, intense period what should
have been established during normal growing up."
William Glasser — (1965) *Reality Therapy*

BACKGROUND

During his residency in the mid-1950s, psychiatrist William Glasser became increasingly frustrated with the psychoanalytic therapy approach as he found patients either unchanged or worsening. Glasser became convinced that mainstream concepts of mental illness and their treatments were essentially useless. In addition, he quickly realized that probing a patient's past to develop insight into present problems was useless. Understanding unconscious conflicts or re-living the past in a transference relationship also were useless. Glasser came to see that maladjusted people all denied reality and appeared unable to fulfill their basic needs in responsible ways. What was missing was individual responsibility for behavior. His first book (Glasser, 1961) outlined the basics of what was later to become *Reality Therapy*.

Noting that almost all therapeutic approaches avoided the concept of morality, Glasser asserted that responsible behavior led to self-worth and fulfillment of needs. A sense of morality — personal responsibility—was the key to appropriate behavior change. Glasser's (1965) text, *Reality Therapy*, essentially espouses a therapy technique where clients are taught how to fulfill basic needs through responsible behavior. Reality therapy techniques are utilized extensively in schools based on Glasser's (1969) book, *Schools Without Failure*.

Glasser's early work with Reality Therapy was mainly with delinquent females. Reality Therapy has been utilized extensively with substance abusers and offenders. His (1984) book, *Control*

Theory, is a self-help form of Reality Therapy that remains in use with criminal justice populations and a client workbook (1990) is available.

DEFINITION IN BRIEF

Reality Therapy is fundamentally a cognitive-behavioral treatment that seeks to have clients achieve control of fulfilling their basic needs through responsible behavior. The primary underlying assumption of the method is that people seek to control their perceptions of reality rather than objective reality itself and that all behavior is an attempt to satisfy basic needs. The method focuses on two aspects of changeable behavior — thinking and actions — and is comprised of three overlapping phases. These are: the exploration of individual perceptions and needs, examining the individual's total behavior, and making plans and commitments toward responsible behavior.

PHILOSOPHY/ASSUMPTIONS/
PERSONALITY THEORY

In his more recent works, Glasser emphasizes that the human brain acts as a control system that satisfies two basic types of needs: *survival* needs (the primary needs that are physiologically based — breathing, reproduction, etc.) and *psychological* needs (belonging, power, fun, and freedom). The "control system" aspect of the brain is genetically based and powerful inborn drives create behavior that seek to satisfy the needs. The brain automatically compares the input it receives with the input it seeks. When perceptual input doesn't match the input the person wants, the person is motivated to perform behaviors that can change the input. Thus, in Reality Therapy, behavior is an attempt to control perceptions in an attempt to make the input received match the input wanted.

Glasser stresses that the survival society of the past has been replaced by an identity society. Individuals in an identity society are "in a search for acceptance as a person" rather than as individuals performing only tasks or fulfilling goals. Most individual human problems stem from failure identities, a circumstance that occurs as individuals fail to achieve self-worth or love. Glasser asserts that individuals who experience only love become dependent on others. Those who experience only worth, eventually find that their achievements are empty of love and they become alienated. Those who fail to achieve both love and self-worth often turn to addictions and various other psychological problems (e.g., somatic symptoms, guilt, anxiety, depression, etc.) as an attempt to control perceptions. Glasser stresses that the maladies and problems that afflict individuals are *chosen* and he/she uses the active form of feelings/behaviors to depict it. For example, an individual may choose drug*ging*, worry-*ing*, headach*ing*, or anxiety*ing* to express that the individual is actively choosing the behavior — they are doing it to themselves. Persons with failure identities are often irrational, lonely, irresponsible, and employing denial of reality. Many with failure identity engage in "pain reduction" behaviors (drug abuse) that foster a sense of immediate gratification. These basic personality traits are developed early in life and lead to maladjusted and irresponsible behavior.

The goal of Reality Therapy is not happiness but rather an acceptance of reality and responsible behavior in our struggles with reality. As clients become more responsible, their self-worth increases. Reality Therapy defines responsible behavior as the ability to fulfill personal needs without depriving others of their ability to fulfill needs (Strupp & Blackwood, 1975).

The relevance of Reality Therapy to treating chemical abusers and offenders is hopefully obvious. Many offenders and substance abusers show failure identities and display impulsive, irresponsible behavior to satisfy immediate gratification needs. The alienation, lack of ability to love and form lasting relationships, and denial employed by such clients points to Reality Therapy as a beneficial treatment option.

TERMINOLOGY & ESSENTIAL KEY CONCEPTS

Control Theory —
The fundamental idea underlying Reality Therapy. The brain is thought of as a control system that makes automatic comparisons between the total sensory and perceptual input received with the total input desired. The brain has pre-established input desired, and when the input received doesn't match that which is desired, the

person is automatically driven to change input. The input received can be changed by defense mechanisms (denial) or through behavior. As behavior is performed, the brain continues to perceive and compare input. For example, an individual who is seeking a job has a desired input (a high-paying, high status job). When the actual input is received by the brain (a low-paying, menial job), the discrepancy between the two leads to behaviors intended to change the input. The person might seek another job, start depressing, anxietying, or failing at the job he or she has. He/she could also blame others, develop a fantasy world, or withdraw into numerous immediate self-gratification behaviors.

BCP —

A basic idea related to control theory that **Behavior Controls** **Perception**.

Perceptual Input —

A person's observations, perceptions, and sensations of how well their basic needs are being fulfilled. All information that the brain senses from outside of self is immediately organized as perceptual input and compared to the desired input.

Needs —

Survival and psychological needs are recognized by Reality Therapy. Survival needs include the preservation of life and limb as well as the need to reproduce. Many of the survival needs are automatically controlled by brain function and modern society has attempted to fulfill much of the survival needs. Psychological needs are as powerful as survival needs and four primary psychological needs exist. These are 1, *belonging* (friends, love, family); 2, *power* (self-worth and recognition); 3, *fun* (play, humor, recreation); 4, *freedom* (ability to make choices).

Identity —

Reality Therapy sees identity as how an individual sees him- or herself in relation with others — it is a social concept. Identity is seen as seeking acceptance as a person of worth and love. Modern society is an identity society rather than a survival society, and a failure identity is one where a person sees the self as a failure in relation to others — self-worth and/or love are not achieved.

Learning —

"We are what we do" is a basic premise of Reality Therapy, and identity is based upon the whole or total of behavior. Much of what we do is learned, and learning new, responsible behavior is a fundamental goal.

Planning —

A fundamental treatment tool in Reality Therapy where the client forms an action plan that is active, relatively simple, and realistically outlines responsible behavior. A contract of commitment to the written plan and a daily log or "performance diary" is typically included in planning.

Meditations —

A positive addiction or daily habit that is developed that assists clients in gaining control that has value, is experienced as satisfying, and easily accomplished. Daily prayer, readings, walking, journaling, and meditation itself are examples.

Confrontation —

Irresponsible behavior has no excuse, thus, all excuses and rationalizations are confronted. Reality Therapy confrontations stress how irresponsible behavior prevents need fulfillment rather than condemnation of the client.

Pinning Down —

A therapist procedure where all of the details of a client's intended responsible behavior are specified by a series of questions. When, where, how, what will you wear, how will you get there are all asked of the client.

COUNSELING PROCESS — In Brief

As with almost all basic counseling theories, Reality Therapy is initiated by listening to the client and showing trust, demonstrating concern for the client, and building a sense of confidence. The focus is on present problems rather than the past, and as clients begin to talk about past events, they are gently guided back to their current problems. Thinking and behavior are the focus since these can be controlled. As feelings emerge in the discussion, the therapist inquires what the client is doing to create these feelings. The therapist provides encouragement to the client that they can gain control and that by not giving up they will eventually be successful.

A client's needs and perceptions are gradually explored. Needs and wants are distinguished and priorities are established. During the process of exploring needs and wants, an evaluation of client behavior occurs in terms of whether their behavior fulfills their needs and wants. While clients will frequently relate the conflicts they have with others, the focus is placed on what the client did in response. A question frequently used by the present authors is, "Did your behavior get you what you wanted?" It is essential that clients evaluate their own behavior rather than a judgement being made by the therapist. As clients come to recognize irresponsible and ineffective behavior, a plan for alternative responsible behaviors can be formed.

The development of a realistic, active, and simple plan is a collaborative effort of therapist-client. Plans may include meditations, journaling, written contracts, and various homework. Client successes are praised and reinforced. Failures are confronted and new plans may be devised. Therapists attempt to have clients become very specific about responsible behaviors committed to in plans by pinning down all of the details.

APPROPRIATE USE/LIMITS

Reality Therapy, correctly performed, is appropriate for the majority of chemical abusers and offenders. Clients in crises, depression, some psychotics, and students have benefitted from the method, but some have cited shortcomings with the approach with minority groups and clients from lower socioeconomic classes. In addition, the system's lack of approaching the past and possible unconscious influences is disturbing to some (Gilliland, et. al., 1994). Perhaps the greatest difficulty that counselors experience with the approach is in the meaning of "reality." Arguments about whose reality is real can often take place — especially with inexperienced counselors. Other arguments about what constitutes responsible behavior and the rightness or wrongness of laws and codes of conduct can take place. In general, counselors with more experience and higher education can maintain the focus on responsible behavior as an appropriate fulfillment of one's needs.

CHAPTER 7
COGNITIVE-BEHAVIOR THERAPY

An almost bewildering number of approaches are cognitive-behavioral in their nature. ... CBT represents a fusion of the best treatment strategies that scientific behavioral psychology has developed with systematic (cognitive) approaches that reshape how clients think and make decisions.
Little — (1992) *Cognitive-Behavioral Treatments Applied To Substance Abusers*

BACKGROUND

Cognitive approaches can be traced to the publication of T. V. Moore's *Cognitive Psychology* (1939) and Kelly's (1955) assertion that *personal constructs* (beliefs) exerted control over feelings and behavior. Ellis' RET, Aaron Beck (1970), and Donald Meichenbaum (1977) subsequently fused basic cognitive concepts with various behavioral procedures to create a unique treatment approach known as cognitive-behavioral therapy (CBT). Beck and Meichenbaum have since become the leading trainers and practitioners advocating CBT applications for depression, anxiety, panic attacks, phobias, and other specific symptomatic disorders. Today, CBT practitioners utilize RET-like sessions combined with tapes and workbooks focused on specific problems. For example, Meichenbaum (1996) has created a videotape and guidebook for mixed depression and anxiety (especially focusing on panic attacks). Greenberger and Padesky's (1995) *Mind Over Mood* focuses on depression, anxiety, anger, guilt, and shame. Little and Robinson (1986; 1988) initially developed MRT® (Moral Reconation Therapy) as a systematic cognitive-behavioral treatment for offenders and substance abusers and subsequently adapted the model in specific workbook strategies for changing beliefs and behaviors regarding clients' parenting skills, job readiness, payment of family support, the development of will power and self-discipline, batterer's treatment, anger management (Little & Robinson, 1991; 1994a, b; 1995a, b; 1997) and relapse prevention (Little, 1997b). The MRT method utilizes tapes, workbooks, and task-oriented guided group sessions.

A major difference between CBT and Ellis' RET lies in practical, systematic guidelines that CBT procedures offer to treatment providers (Gilliland, et. al., 1994). In addition, some CBT approaches utilizing workbooks and standardized, sequential procedures, require less training and education for therapists, and are amenable to mass treatment where program participants may move from site to site. For example, in an article and earlier interview in *Correctional Health Care Management*, Waggoner (1994) explained why the CBT approach of MRT was adapted to an entire state prison system: MRT was directly designed for substance abusing offenders, was conducted in open-ended groups where offenders could be transferred from one facility or level of supervision to another and continue at the same place they left off, required minimal training, held staff and participants accountable, led to measurable change, and was "user friendly." The MRT model has been adapted by several states' criminal justice systems and has been used on approximately 100,000 offenders in over 30 states. Outcome data on MRT, measuring rearrests and reincarcerations on nearly 6,000 treated offenders in several states (in prisons, jails, parole/probation, and rehabilitation residential programs), has shown that treated offenders show 25% to 90% lower recidivism than controls up to seven years after treatment (Little, Robinson, Burnette, & Swan, 1996 reviewed all of this data). It is likely that cognitive-behavioral interventions have had more scientific outcome data supporting their effectiveness on substance abusers and offenders than any other approach.

Another minor difference between CBT and RET lies in the influence of biological predispositions on behavior. RET assumes that the vast majority of behavior is biological while CBT acknowledges the biological influence, but views it as much smaller. Finally, RET is more of a general approach to all human problems and disorders while CBT methods tend to be highly focused on clusters of symptoms surrounding a core disorder.

DEFINITION IN BRIEF

Cognitive-behavioral therapies seek to make people aware of their irrational and negative thinking, self-defeating and self-reinforcing inappropriate behavior, and to replace them with rational thinking and appropriate, goal-oriented, effective behaviors. The approach utilizes both cognitive and behavioral methodologies and represents a sequential, systematic approach to treat selective client problems.

PHILOSOPHY/ASSUMPTIONS/ PERSONALITY THEORY

Cognitive-behavioral theory asserts that beliefs and cognitions produce feelings and behaviors in the same way that RET asserts. It is how an individual views an activating event, their beliefs about the event, that leads to their feelings and behavior. For example, in a simplistic sense, if a person believes that they are depressed or expect to be depressed because of some external event, they subsequently feel and act depressed. The feelings and behavior indicating depression then serve to confirm the belief that they are depressed. *You are what you do*, is a basic premise of CBT. This self-reinforcing cycle is attacked by CBT in a two-pronged approach: 1) the cognitions and irrational beliefs are challenged and disputed, and 2) behavioral techniques and methods are employed to alter behavioral responses.

Meichenbaum's (1996) explanation of how panic attacks occur is relevant. Meichenbaum relates that research shows that about 75% of panic attacks are "triggered" by an external event (activating event). The external triggering event can be many different things ranging from witnessing an argument to getting out of breath after climbing a flight of stairs. The individual then quickly "appraises" the situation based on their beliefs. Those who experience panic attacks tend to appraise "neutral" situations unduly as a threat. After the situation is viewed as threatening ("This is dangerous; It may cause a heart attack"), feelings emerge with the "automatic thoughts" of threats and fear. Next, a series of bodily sensations occur that rapidly cause an increase in fear with anxiety (hyperventilation, shakiness, lightheadedness) followed by what is termed a "catastrophic misinterpretation" ("I'm having a heart attack" or "I'm losing control"). This, in turn, causes more severe feelings of apprehension followed by more severe bodily sensations, and so on. With panic attacks, the cycle (beliefs - feelings - body sensations - misinterpretation - more severe feelings - worse bodily sensations) turns quickly until the individual experiences a full-blown panic attack where they have all the outward signs of a heart attack. Treatment involves changing the client's beliefs and interpretations of such events while also employing behavioral methods (e.g. relaxation, teaching coping skills) that directly counteract the symptoms.

CBT practitioners view the personality as the total structure of beliefs learned through social and other means. Emotions, feelings, and behavior are results of how an individual perceives events. An individual's beliefs determine their perceptions and subsequent interpretations. That is, many people selectively perceive events that confirm their pre-existing beliefs. Thus, beliefs can "predispose" individuals to specific disorders. Beck has referred to this as a form of *"cognitive vulnerability."* Problems can stem from irrational beliefs, distorted perceptions, inadequate or poor reasoning, selective attention or inattention, and other cognitive distortions. MRT theorizes that *inadequate moral reasoning* is a major cause of self-destructive, hedonistic behavior and addictions (Little & Robinson, 1988) and the method significantly raises moral reasoning.

Numerous behavioral strategies are today considered to be under the wide umbrella of CBT. These include desensitization and relaxation training, dysfunctional thoughts' logging, imagery, homework, journaling, behavioral rehearsal & practice, thought stopping, neurolinguistic programming, and biofeedback. Little (1992) emphasizes that CBT interventions are characterized by seven primary elements: **1) they are based on behavioral psychology learning principles; 2) the focus is on changing thinking and behavior; 3) they obviously and directly relate to the problems and difficulties of the client; 4) they are systematic with a prescribed sequence of therapeutic interventions used in a prescribed fashion at a prescribed time; 5) they are relatively short-term; 6) they represent a blend of active exercises, tasks, homework, and skills building; 7) are backed by scientific outcome research and make alterations based on findings.**

TERMINOLOGY &
ESSENTIAL KEY CONCEPTS

Many of the strategies employed in CBT utilize RET concepts and methods including irrational beliefs, disputing and challenging irrational beliefs, ABC theory, and client education. In addition, many of the strategies presented in the behavioral counseling chapter are also utilized including relaxation training, systematic desensitization, homework, and contracting. *It should be understood and stressed again that CBT practitioners often use specific procedures and techniques designed especially to treat specific problems* (e.g., depression, offender rehabilitation, chemical abuse, parenting, job readiness, anger control, etc.). Specific workbooks and training materials are typically employed with such CBT methods. In his meta-analysis of approximately 1000 published outcome studies, Andrews (1994) listed eight characteristics of effective interventions for offenders. These were: cognitive-behavioral interventions, the use of printed programming manuals/workbooks, they address criminal thinking and needs, are empirically validated on criminals, the staff is specifically trained in the method, the staff is enthusiastic and understands Antisocial Personality Disorder, problem solving and skills building are the focus, and structured follow-ups are provided to participants. Correctional treatment authorities are all calling for the utilization of specific CBT approaches on drug-abusing offenders.

Imagery exercises —

CBT approaches use imagery in desensitization, as a form of cognitive practice and rehearsal, to visualize a positive future, to visualize success, and prepare for situations. Imagery is typically done with the client in a state of relaxation and is a treatment adjunct with batterer's treatment (to facilitate "time-outs" and relaxation), with anger management, and in relapse prevention, as well as with depression, anxiety, and phobias.

Journaling —

As with Reality Therapy, journaling is sometimes developed as a positive daily habit in CBT that can be useful in charting irrational thoughts and behaviors, activating events, assist clients to understand the connection between beliefs and emotions/behavior, and provide information to the therapist.

Thought stopping —

Patients who show powerful and debilitating irrational thoughts and obsessions, can often respond to this technique. The extreme method of yelling "stop" can serve as a powerful interruption to unwanted thoughts.

Biofeedback —
Providing clients, especially those with anxiety disorders or anger control problems, with feedback on their physiological arousal state can be useful. Some CBT practitioners employ biofeedback techniques for this.

Cognitive restructuring —
Teaches clients to replace debilitating, self-defeating, and absolute beliefs with more appropriate, less absolute beliefs. While cognitive restructuring employs many additional techniques, one method has the client rate events on a 1-10 scale. For example, a client may say that being in jail is a 10 — totally awful. The therapist may ask the client "what could be worse or more awful?" While the client might say "nothing," it could then be asked, "if you had been in a wreck and were a quadriplegic, would that be worse than jail?" "What if you had a life sentence, would that be worse?" When the client says, "yes, that would be worse," the therapist might say, now, if getting a life sentence would be a 10, the worst thing that could happen, where is your current jail sentence on our 1-10 scale?" At this point, clients might reply, "an eight." While the method goes beyond this simple example, it can be seen that what the client originally believed was totally awful, was restructured — the method altered the client's perception so that it is no longer seen as awful — the worst possible event.

Moral Reconation Therapy - MRT® —
A systematic, trademarked CBT method that has designed specific workbooks and procedures for a variety of problems seen in treatment-resistant populations. Substance abuse and offender MRT consists of 12 steps characterized by exercises and tasks performed as homework and then shared in groups. The group leader typically passes clients who complete the step's exercises and tasks as measured by objective criteria. The method has its own personality theory and different workbooks for different populations (e.g., adults, juveniles, batterers, anger, parenting, etc.). The method addresses moral reasoning, decision making, and faulty, irrational beliefs throughout its sequential process. Rational and effective behaviors as well as vari-

ous skills training are built into the process. MRT was initially developed as drug treatment for drug offenders within a prison context and has gradually expanded to general offender rehabilitation as well as retaining its drug/alcohol treatment origins. The approach is performed in groups that can be performed in outpatient and inpatient settings and meshes and blends with other program components. The MRT batterer treatment workbook consists of sequential modules that focus on power and control beliefs and behaviors commonly seen in this offender group. The relapse prevention version also utilizes sequential modules specifically focusing on relapse issues.

COUNSELING PROCESS — In Brief

There is no one counseling process that describes CBT approaches. Beck's CBT approach for depression characterizes one form of the process. In this method the therapist and client develop a relationship through therapist listening, understanding, and the development of trust, warmth, and acceptance. One goal of the relationship is to foster a client expectancy of success as well as confidence in the skills of the therapist. The therapist assists the client in identifying the circumstances and conditions (activating events) that can serve as markers for depression, anxiety, panic attacks, etc. At the same time, clients are encouraged to "discover" their cognitions, beliefs, and assumptions that are related to their problematic behavior/symptoms. Gradually, clients are taught to recognize and appropriately respond to both internal and external cues that signal problems. Various behavioral techniques like relaxation training, systematic desensitization, and imagery are employed to teach the client coping skills. The method of stress inoculation is also employed wherein clients practice stress recognition and reduction methods between sessions.

Some CBT approaches consist of workbooks and manuals that focus on clusters of symptoms primarily in group settings. MRT, for example, requires clients to complete homework assignments prior to each session and groups are conducted for each client to present their work. Some homework consists of client drawings in response to specific questions. The counselor's role is to gently but firmly motivate participants to successfully complete the modules or steps based on objective criteria. In such programming, the counselor is taught to be caring and develop trust with clients by being consistent and reliable. That is, by following the instructions and objective criteria, clients are ensured that they will pass each assignment. Thus, development of a personal relationship with a particular counselor is not stressed or particularly important. Counselors in these groups are task oriented and facilitate client self-discovery and participation with each client's group presentation. Clients engaged in the process at one site can transfer to another site and enter another MRT group (with a different counselor), and continue with treatment at the same basic point where they left off. MRT's basic format sequentially guides clients through exercises designed to foster honesty, trust, acceptance, awareness, responsibility for relationships, development of social skills, development of appropriate goals, establishing an action plan for goals, maintenance of the action plan, fostering a deeper self-discovery of self and relationships, and understanding the relationships between goals, self-worth, and happiness in a social world.

APPROPRIATE USE/LIMITS

Cognitive-behavioral treatments have provided counselors with some of the most powerful treatment tools and technologies available. Clearly, CBT is the preferred treatment approach for depression, anxiety, panic attacks, and a host of other disorders. Offender treatment with CBT is especially effective as substantial outcome research indicates. CBT offers problem-specific systematic programs for a host of offender problems including anger control, substance abuse, relapse prevention, job readiness, social skills, etc. One other consistent finding has been the satisfaction that counseling staff utilizing CBT approaches experience. Counselors in criminal justice settings and many counselors treating chemical dependency often experience frustration and discouragement with more traditional counseling approaches. CBT provides them with a task-oriented, systematic process that seems to relieve pressure while producing observable and measurable beneficial changes in clients.

CBT is especially amenable with minority populations, resistant clients, and the disabled (Gilliland, et. al., 1994). The method may be least useful with clients experiencing normal grief and when counselors insist that the past causes current problems or when the goal is to "work through" feelings.

CHAPTER 8
GESTALT THERAPY

Anybody who goes to a therapist has something up his sleeve. I would say
roughly ninety percent don't go to a therapist to be cured, but to be more
adequate in their neurosis. If they are power mad, they want to get more
power. If they are intellectual, they want to have more elephantshit. If they
are ridiculers, they want to have a sharper wit to ridicule, and so on...
Fritz Perls — (1969) *Gestalt Therapy Verbatim*

BACKGROUND

While Gestalt Therapy is associated with psychiatrist Fritz
Perls, Gestalt psychology actually developed in Germany in the
early 1910s and thus greatly influenced its later development. Gestalt
psychology emerged as a result of Albert Einstein's field theory
profoundly impressing the psychologists Kurt Koffka, Max
Wertheimer, and Wolfgang Kohler. Gestalt psychology is known for
asserting that, *the whole is greater than the sum of its parts* (Thetford &
Schucman, 1975; Strupp & Blackwood, 1975). The German word
gestalt essentially means "**whole**."

Perls, as happened with many other psychoanalyists, became
disenchanted with Freudian treatment concepts and developed a
positive view of human potentials. Perls strongly asserted that
nothing exists but the present moment — the *now* — and that focusing on the past was a way of avoiding the present. Furthermore,
thinking and planning about the future could cause anxiety and also
avoided the present. Perls also found that many patients sought to
talk about their feelings rather than actually fully *experience* them
resulting in a word game that led nowhere. Many problems came
from avoiding personal responsibility in the present by blaming the
past, living in the past or future, and through other blocks to
awareness that keep the individual from being totally alive.

Gestalt Therapy is an existential, humanistic, and holistic
therapy that has pieced together the theories and methods of various

other theorists including Otto Rank and Wilhelm Reich. The totality of the individual — body and spirit, our existence in the present, ever-changing moment, and our innate ability to grow to maturity are philosophical underpinnings of the method.

Perl's (1947) book, *Ego, Hunger, and Aggression* represented his initial formulations of Gestalt Therapy. After moving to the United States in 1947, Perls was influenced by the human potential movement, and subsequently coauthored *Gestalt Therapy: Excitement and Growth in the Human Personality* (Perls, Hefferline, & Goodman, 1951) followed by numerous other publications. Today, various Gestalt Therapy institutes exist. The method has been employed with substance abusers and offenders, however, Gestalt theory has long down-played the importance of objective outcome studies (Strupp & Blackwood, 1975).

DEFINITION IN BRIEF

Gestalt Therapy assists clients to fully experience their total "being" in the present by bringing into the clients' awareness the methods they employ to prevent themselves from experiencing the here-and-now. A variety of techniques are employed to facilitate awareness of the present. With this fundamental awareness of their total being, clients can effectively deal with life problems by becoming personally responsible for their personal integration and growth.

PHILOSOPHY/ASSUMPTIONS/ PERSONALITY THEORY

All human beings are in a constant struggle to maintain their balance, a *homeostasis*, as internal and external forces frequently create tension. For example, as a need (e.g., hunger) is perceived by an individual, the homeostasis (balance) is disturbed causing an instinctual motivation to satisfy the need and re-establish homeostasis. A healthy person is able to recognize their needs in the present moment and fulfill them through responsible behavior. Once fulfilled, a need recedes into the background with another need soon moving to the forefront. The ability to clearly differentiate between important needs (the central *figure* in the individual's total field of experience and being) and needs in the background (*ground*) are a hallmark of maturity. *Maladjustment and psychological problems develop when an individual can't sharply clarify figure from ground.* Their gestalt (total field of being) is cluttered creating confusion, uncertainty, and low awareness of the present. Gestalt Therapy asserts that such people often attempt to actualize an *image* of self rather than the real self. Such individuals manipulate self and others, try to control situations that are not under their control, and resist change. Anxiety is created by preoccupation with the future.

The homeostatic balance mechanism working through awareness of the total gestalt of figure-ground represents a form of perceptual organizing leading to need fulfillment and expression of affect. Both physiological (survival; reproduction) and psychological needs (love, sharing, belonging, etc.) create tensions and cause unbalance. Perls believed that modern society was sick — insane — and that centering on self was the only sane course of action. This centering was accomplished by becoming totally aware in the present moment. Modern civilization creates a "split" in personality because of its emphasis on self-control — unmet needs are repressed and behavior that could meet these needs is controlled — but, the control is faulty since the needs remain cluttered in the background causing confusion. However, some people "act out" inappropriately as the ability to fully suppress needs and behavior doesn't ever completely work. Thus, the discovery of unmet needs and their expression in the here-and-now — leading to full awareness — is the fundamental curative process of Gestalt Therapy.

One of the major concepts in Gestalt Therapy is *unfinished business*. Unfinished business represents **unexpressed, lingering feelings**—usually anger, resentment, pain, guilt, grief, abandonment, etc. — that resulted from psychological needs that were unfulfilled. Although they have receded into the background, **unfinished business exerts a nagging block of growth** to maturity and reaching full awareness. Gestalt Therapy seeks to have clients get unstuck by creating *closure* on unfinished business by expressing the unacknowledged and poorly understood feelings in the present moment. Usually unfinished business relates to specific events and interactions with others. Rather than having the client simply relate the event, they relive it and express their feelings in the present. A variety of techniques are employed in this endeavor with Gestalt Therapy being most amenable to group settings.

TERMINOLOGY &
ESSENTIAL KEY CONCEPTS

It is important to understand and keep in mind that Gestalt techniques and concepts all relate to experiencing in the present. Many Gestalt methods are powerful and can result in sudden expressions of emotions and feelings that inexperienced counselors may be unprepared to handle. Gestalt therapists utilize a number of techniques to facilitate awareness of the present and most of them are employed in groups.

Homeostasis —
The striving for maintaining balance, a sense of equilibrium, is served by recognition of needs and their fulfillment. The ability to distinguish important present needs, fulfill them, and allow them to recede into the background is a hallmark of maturity. From this perspective, the ability to maintain homeostasis is mature, responsible behavior.

Responsibility —
The idea that every person determines and creates their own existence — each of us is the master of our fate. Acceptance and fulfillment of responsibility is a Gestalt goal.

Figure-Ground —
The saying, "you can't see the forest for the trees" is one analogy to figure-ground. In Gestalt theory, both figure and ground are equally important since both comprise the "whole" or the **total** gestalt. A person who focuses on figure (the trees) misses the bigger picture and loses awareness of fundamental aspects of self. For example, a person who totally focuses on their future goals misses the present. Focusing on a past event also leads to missing the present. At the same time, it is necessary to differentiate the important figures (needs) as they come to the forefront from less important needs and other issues in the background. An individual may be unable to fulfill their present needs because they are attending to all of the *unfinished business* (the clutter) in the background.

Unfinished Business —

Unresolved and unexpressed feelings that linger in the background creating interference with responsible behavior and contact with others. Often considered to be "emotional debris" or "baggage" clients carry with them, unfinished business produces sticking points in growth.

Dialogue Game —

Often utilizes the *"empty chair technique"* to resolve a basic conflict in opposing parts of a client's personality. Two chairs are placed in the center of the room with the client sitting in one chair playing the role of a "critical parent" — the authoritarian, dogmatic, bossy part of the personality. After expressing the feelings of the critical parent side of their personality (also called the *top dog*), the client moves to the other chair and plays the role of the "apologetic child" (also called the *underdog*) — the helpless, weak, defensive, victim's part of their personality. Clients are encouraged to genuinely experience and fully express the feelings in each role. The method is also used to raise awareness of unfinished business as well as other issues.

Making The Rounds —

A group technique where a person is requested to speak directly to each group member individually. Varying forms of the method exist often with a sentence completion. For example, each member might have to say, "I can't trust you because..." or "What I like about you is..." to every member of the group.

I Have A Secret —

One of the most powerful Gestalt techniques involving group members' secrets. Without revealing a secret they have brought into their awareness, each group member states what others might say to them if they knew the secret.

Reversal Technique —

Used to assist clients to become aware of parts of themselves that have been denied. For example, the shy group member is requested to role play an outgoing, flamboyant person in group by acting outlandish and speaking without inhibitions.

Stay With The Feeling —

When expressing unpleasant or painful feelings, some clients will quickly move to other topics avoiding experiencing the feelings in the here-and-now. They are told to "stay with the feelings" and to experience them.

The Hot Seat —

A technique where a client sits in the middle of the group and is confronted by the therapist and group members.

Dream Work —

Gestalt dream work is one of the most interesting and enlightening of all its methods. Rather than interpreting dreams, Gestalt dream work involves bringing the dream "to life." Each element in the dream represents a part of the client's Gestalt, and by acting out that part, by becoming every part of the dream, often one by one, awareness of various aspects of personality is increased.

COUNSELING PROCESS — In Brief

Gestalt therapists begin the counseling process by listening to client statements about their problems and gaining their trust and confidence. The here-and-now focus is emphasized in initial sessions, even when clients relate past events, "How do you feel about that right now?" is often queried. As unfinished business and other blocks to the client's awareness become evident, "experiments" are conducted utilizing any Gestalt technique that facilitates the expression of feelings in the present. Often, clients are encouraged to enter ongoing Gestalt groups.

During the counseling process, clients discover how to distinguish their present needs and wants from the background. "What do you want right now?" is frequently asked. Gestalt therapy is active in that clients are motivated and encouraged to participate in various "games" and other techniques that help them discover denied and unfulfilled parts of themselves. The therapist is spontaneous and tries various techniques (games) as experiments. For example, if a client is shy in group, the therapist might say, "let's try a little experiment here. I'd like you make a statement to each person in this group. Finish this sentence: 'I am afraid to trust you because...'

" Although it hasn't been stressed in this chapter, nonverbal behavior (body language) is also an important element in Gestalt Therapy. The therapist may employ a variety of methods, especially exaggeration, to elucidate feelings underlying body language.

Obviously, client trust and confidence in the group itself is extremely important. In addition, counselor expertise, comfort in facing and handling strong feelings, and an accepting, non-condemning attitude are essential.

APPROPRIATE USE/LIMITS

Many counselors employ Gestalt techniques at times when faced with clients that refuse to or can't seem to deal with the present. Few, if any, substance abuse programs exclusively employ the therapy as their primary drug treatment method. However, as experienced counselors will attest, many Gestalt techniques are useful and some counselors in private practice maintain Gestalt-oriented groups. Gestalt is most appropriate with clients who have at least average intellectual ability, are experiencing a crisis, with individuals who lack direction, and with multicultural groups. One problem with Gestalt groups is that the counselor can become a "guru" with the group members becoming dependent. This situation can eventually build resentments and move the focus from clients to therapist. Another problem can occur with the philosophy that the individual totally creates his or her reality. Some clients may resist this philosophy and argue that social interactions and other circumstances have produced their difficulties. Overcoming this resistance can be difficult for some types of clients and problems. Finally, it should be understood that very little objective outcome data exists on Gestalt methods — especially on chemical abusers and offenders.

CHAPTER 9
TRANSACTIONAL ANALYSIS

Man is born free, but one of the first things he learns is to do as he is
told, and he spends the rest of his life doing that. Thus, his first
enslavement is to his parents. He follows their instructions
forevermore, retaining only in some cases the right to choose
his own methods and consoling himself
with an illusion of autonomy.
Eric Berne— (1970) *Sex in Human Loving*

BACKGROUND

Eric Berne, a psychoanalytically-trained psychiatrist, gradually became frustrated with the slowness of psychoanalysis during his early practice. During World War II, Berne conducted over 40,000 psychiatric evaluations on discharged soldiers with each evaluation lasting 90 seconds. As a mental game, he began trying to guess the civilian occupation of each soldier. He found that he could accurately guess farmers and mechanics — but that was all. Gradually he developed the ability to raise his accuracy and then became fascinated by the remarkable ability of carnival weight-guessers. He believed that a form of intuition was developed early in life that appeared able to accurately reality test using various nonvocal clues and other information. He also discovered that people developed what he termed primal images — a sort of evaluative judgement that immediately classified other people based on a combination of intuition and rational observations. This early work, conducted in the late 1940s and 1950s, led Berne to understand that the ego was actually comprised of three separate states (Dusay, 1975).

Berne subsequently published his ego state theory in 1957 followed by the book, *Transactional Analysis in Psychotherapy* (1961), outlining the use of the ego states as an adjunct in group therapy. In the 1960s, two books, *Games People Play* (Berne, 1964) and *I'm OK — You're OK* (Harris, 1969) led to an enormous popularity of the rapidly developing Transactional Analysis (TA). Numerous other best-selling books were published on TA (e.g. *Born To Win* and *What Do You Say After You Say Hello*) that continued its popularity.

TA is used by many counselors with substance abusers and delinquents. Many therapists find the TA concepts of ego states (child, adult, parent) to be useful with clients and the analysis of client life positions very helpful. The TA concept of scripting, a life-plan developed early in life that determines the person's life position in relation to others has great relevance with clients that experience depression, frustration, negativity, or paranoia.

TA derives its underpinning from Freudian psychoanalysis and utilizes behavioral and humanistic techniques. In addition, much like Gestalt Therapy, TA tends to take a here-and-now perspective and is most effective in group settings.

DEFINITION IN BRIEF

Transactional Analysis is an active therapeutic process where clients assess themselves and others and come to understand how their present feelings and behavior are related to ego states developed early in life. These ego states determine a repetitive pattern of behavior called a life script that determines a fundamental position in life — how they view themselves in relation to others. TA carefully analyzes transactions between people's ego states to discover overt and hidden psychological meanings and uncovers behavioral and emotional patterns individuals employ in playing "games" with others to receive desired responses. Fully understanding their life position, their frequently used games, and early life script, clients are freed to make decisions regarding a new script.

PHILOSOPHY/ASSUMPTIONS/ PERSONALITY THEORY

TA's personality theory is derived, in large part, from Freudian theory. Infants are stroked, cuddled, and held by parents giving the infant a sense of acceptance or rejection. The first ego state, the *Child*, develops as a consequence of how often the infant's impulsive behaviors (e.g., sucking, crying, etc.) result in *strokes* — reinforcers from other people, especially parents. Aggression, of major interest in TA, develops early in life and is related to specific infant behavior (biting, chewing). The *Adult* ego state begins its development with verbal language. The Adult ego state serves to make conscious decisions regarding how the needs and wants of the Child are fulfilled. As the child receives strokes for various behaviors and emotions — or is discouraged from acting or feeling in certain ways — their *life script* and *life position* begin to form as a rudimentary conscious decision. During this same time, the *Parent* ego state also develops wherein the child absorbs beliefs, behaviors, and emotions that play a role in the choice of life script and life position. The Adult ego state then serves as a mediator between the urges and impulses of the Child, and the restrictions and admonitions of the Parent.

The life position adopted by the child relates to how they perceive and interact with others and influences the life script. A "winner's life script" comes from having needs met and experiencing acceptance and love. This position is called *I'm OK — You're OK*. Some children experience abuse or mistreatment and begin to blame others as they become suspicious. This position results in paranoia and anger and is called the *I'm OK — You're Not OK* position. Children who receive negative strokes or too few strokes, develop a sense of futility resulting in a *I'm Not OK — You're Not OK* position. The most frequent life position adopted is one where the person blames him- or herself for not fulfilling needs. This *I'm Not OK — You're OK* position results in depression and feelings of inadequacy.

As they move through life interacting with others, individuals assume any of the three ego states — Parent, Child, Adult — and combinations of them as they socialize and receive responses in return (transactions). TA analyzes these transactions, the ego states involved, and the life position on social levels and deeper psychological levels.

Maladjustment comes from adopting any of the life positions except the winner's position and by following the life script blindly. Part of the TA process involves identifying the consistent games people play on the deeper psychological level (called *rackets*) and helping the client understand them and then choose to free themselves of it. The goals of TA are to educate the client in TA terminology, raise their awareness and understanding of their interactions with others, make their life position and life script fully conscious, and then guide them through a redecision process.

TERMINOLOGY &
ESSENTIAL KEY CONCEPTS

Ego States —

Represent three possible states or conditions of the personality each with its own unified system of behavior patterns, thoughts, and feelings. These ego states are child, parent, and adult.

Child Ego State —

Contains the cumulation of all early life experiences, positions taken with others and the responses received, and behaviors. The child ego state is impulsive and spontaneous and has two primary types: The *free child* is a playful, spontaneous, impulsive, and curious state. The *adapted child* is either yielding or disobedient. The Child ego state serves as the primary motivator throughout life.

Parent Ego State —

The totality of a person's *chosen* thoughts, emotions, and behaviors that lead to acting as a **nurturing parent** (warmth and support) or **critical parent** (controlling). The Parent ego state is also divided into three parts: Parent, Adult, and Child.

Adult Ego State —

The part of the ego that serves as the decision-maker in regards to the wants of the Child and the restrictions of the Parent.

Transaction —

An exchange — or form of communication — between one person's ego state with another person's ego state. It is conceived as a stimulus-response exchange between ego states. When the transaction is **manifest,** it is typically a direct verbal response with a specific, easily understood meaning. A transaction can also have a *latent* or hidden meaning that can be observed in both verbal and nonverbal behavior. Three primary types of transactions exist.

Complementary Transaction —

When a transaction occurs between two persons' identical ego states, it is said to be complementary. For example, when the adult ego state of one person asks a question of another person

("When are we leaving?"), and receives a reply from the adult ego state of the other person ("Four o'clock.") it is complementary. **In complementary transactions, communication between the two people can continue.**

Crossed Transaction —

When a transaction occurs between two different ego states it is crossed. For example, when the adult ego state of one person asks a question of another person ("When are we leaving?"), and receives a reply from the parent ego state of the other person ("When I say so."). In crossed transactions, arguments and hurt feelings often ensue.

Ulterior Transaction —

When a transaction between two people simultaneously contains manifest and latent meaning, it is said to be *ulterior*. Both *social* and *psychological* communications are present in ulterior transactions. For example, when one person's adult ego state asks a question of another person ("What time are we leaving?"), and the other person's adult ego state replies, "That all depends," there is a hidden meaning. The hidden meaning may come from a playful interchange between the child ego states of the two people playing *games*.

Games —

Games represent repeating transactions between people with ulterior motives. On a surface, social level, games often appear to be exchanges between adult ego states, but under the surface, at the deeper psychological level, the child of one person can be interacting with the parent or child ego state of the other. The underlying motive of games is to receive *strokes*. Berne lists 36 standard types of *Games People Play* (1964).

Strokes —

Most human behavior is motivated by strokes — essentially reinforcements or rewards from others. At a primal level, strokes are physical (like a mother cuddling and gently patting her baby). Other positive strokes are verbal praise and approval. Strokes can also be negative ("You are really stupid"), because it is believed that negative strokes are better than no strokes. People play games and develop *rackets* to achieve strokes when they cannot receive them in a direct fashion.

Rackets —

A person's favorite game, and its associated feeling, represent an individual's racket. Rackets are utilized by the person to verify and reinforce their *life position.* Rackets are believed to be learned early in life from parents (usually only one parent) and represent the cumulative negative feelings of the person. As negative feelings arise from rackets, the individual "collects them" like trading stamps. When a sufficient number of **stamps** have been collected by the person, they can act out in small or large ways (yelling, killing) and feel justification.

Life Position —

Typically, a person's life position comes from how an individual's feelings as a child were responded to by their parents. The life position plays a major role in the development of the individual's life *script.* There are four major life positions: 1) *I'm OK — You're OK.* This is referred to as the **winner's script** resulting from having needs met and sufficient strokes delivered; 2) *I'm OK — You're Not OK.* This is referred to as the **paranoid script** resulting from blame of others for unjust treatment; 3) *I'm Not OK — You're OK.* This is referred to as the **depression script** resulting from self blame for not receiving strokes; 4) *I'm Not OK — You're Not OK.* This is referred to as the **futile script** because the person has given up the attempt to receive strokes.

Scripts —

An individual's plan of life developed in childhood that has a mythic or fairy-tale quality to it. Scripts come from parental influences and demands that are sometimes contradictory, moralistic, idealistic, or defeating. When childhood strokes are conditional — based on performance of some behavior or parental approval — scripts become limiting and retard individual growth. A major focus of TA is to change clients' life scripts to the winner's script or to have no script at all. This changing of the life script is referred to as the **redecision** process.

Drama Triangle —

A TA game frequently encountered in clients involving a **victim** (futile script), a **rescuer** (a sympathetic ear), and a **persecutor** (seen as superior). Understanding and escaping drama triangles is important for clients entangled in one. Enacting the drama triangle in a group setting is done to teach the concept.

Discounting —

A way of avoiding problems and confirming the life position that takes place in four ways. The **existence** or **significance** of problems can be down-played or denied. Stating that the problem is **out of their control** is another form of discounting. The person can also discount their **ability** to change the problem.

COUNSELING PROCESS — In Brief

TA therapists typically create and continue to modify a contract with clients starting at the beginning of treatment. Based on the client's presenting problem and initial desired changes, the counselor specifies the initial goals and how they will be addressed. For example, if a client stated, "I want to quit using drugs and develop positive work habits," the contract will specify those goals and state, in brief, the initial activities that the client will participate in including the where, hows, and other details. This is a joint effort between therapist-client. Readings on TA are often assigned to clients in the first sessions including *Born To Win, I'm OK — You're OK,* and *Games People Play.*

Most TA clients participate in ongoing groups. In groups, TA terminology (e.g., ego positions, life positions, strokes, rackets, games, discounting, etc.) are heavily employed. Thus, the therapist educates clients on the terminology and relies on clients to read assigned materials. TA groups are active and employ various Gestalt techniques to bring feelings and thoughts into the present. A version of the empty chair technique is used as are numerous other methods. Therapists move clients from one technique to another as appropriate based on observations and intuitions. A heavy emphasis on analysis of transactions occurs with the goal of making the client fully aware of them. As a client's awareness increases, a redecision process is employed to have the client write a new life script or free themselves from them.

APPROPRIATE USE/LIMITS

TA is considered to be a multicultural approach that recognizes the influence of family — a critical issue to many cultures. People who are involved in alcohol recovery groups like Adult Children of Alcoholics find the technique and its terminology useful. In addition, the terminology of TA lends itself to an in-depth personal and interpersonal analysis. At the same time, some counselors and clients become so indoctrinated by TA terminology that they find it difficult to perform other approaches utilizing other terms. Finally, clients with below average mental abilities may find it difficult to grasp the terminology, the deeper meanings underlying transactions, and fail to understand the concepts of scripts and life position.

REFERENCES

ACA (1996) *1996 Membership Directory*. White Plains, NY: Harris Publ. Co.

Andrews, D. A. (1994) An Overview of Treatment Effectiveness: Research and Clinical Principles. In: *What Works: Bridging the Gap Between Research and Correctional Practice*. Longmont, CO: National Institute of Corrections.

Bandura, A. (1969) *Principles of Behavior Modification*. NY: Holt, Rinehart, & Winston.

Beck, A. T. (1970) Cognitive therapy: nature and relation to behavior therapy. *Behavior Therapy*, 1, 184-200.

Bekhterev, V. M. (1912) Die Anwendung der Methode der motorischen Assoziations-reflexe zur Aufdeckung der Simulation. *Z. gesamte Neurol. Psychiatry*, 13, 183.

Berne, E. (1957) The ego image. *Psychiatric Quarterly*, 31, 611.

Berne, E. (1961) *Transactional Analysis in Psychotherapy*. New York: Grove Press.

Berne, E. (1964) *Games People Play*. New York: Grove Press.

Bradley, F. O. (Ed.) (1991) *Credentialing in Counseling.*Alexandria, VA: AACD.

Brecher, E. M. (1972) *Licit & Illicit Drugs*. Boston: Little, Brown & Co.

Brown, B. S. (1975) Definition of mental health and disease.

In: A. M. Freedman, H. I. Kaplan, & B. J. Sadock (Eds.) *Comprehensive Textbook of Psychiatry — II.* Baltimore: Williams & Wilkins, Pp. 2324-2326.

Bufe, C. Q. (1991) *Alcoholics Anonymous: Cult or Cure.* San Francisco: See Sharp Press.

Chaplin, J. P. (1975) *Dictionary of Psychology.* New York: Laurel.

Corey, G. (1977) *Theory and Practice of Counseling and Psychotherapy.* Monterey, CA: Brooks/Cole.

Cottle, W. C., & Downie, N. M. (1970) *Preparation for Counseling.* Englewood Cliffs, NJ: Prentice-Hall.

Crowe, A. H., & Reeves, R. (1994) *Treatment for Alcohol and Other Drug Abuse.* Rockville, MD: Center for Substance Abuse Treatment.

DeLong, J. V. (1972) Treatment and Rehabilitation. In: *Dealing With Drug Abuse: A Report to the Ford Foundation.* New York: Praeger.

Drake, R. E., & Mueser, K. T. (1996) Alcohol-use disorder and severe mental illness. *Alcohol Health & Research World,* 20, 87-94.

Drug Abuse Survey Project (1972) *Dealing With Drug Abuse: A Report to the Ford Foundation.* New York: Praeger.

Dusay, J. M. (1975) Eric Berne. In: A. M. Freedman, H. I. Kaplan, & B. J. Sadock (Eds.) *Comprehensive Textbook of Psychiatry — II.* Baltimore: Williams & Wilkins, Pp. 619-625.

Eidelberg, L. (Ed.) (1968) *Encyclopedia of Psychoanalysis.* Toronto: Collier-MacMillan.

Ellis, A. (1970) Rational-emotive therapy. In: R. Corsini (Ed.) *Current Psychotherapies.* Itasca, IL: Peacock.

Ellis, A. (1991) Introduction. In: Bufe, C. Q. *Alcoholics Anonymous: Cult or Cure.* San Francisco: See Sharp Press.

Ellis, A., McInerney, J. F., DiGiuseppe, R., & Yeager, R. J. (1988) *Rational-Emotive Therapy With Alcoholics and Substance Abusers.* Boston: Allyn & Bacon.

Franks, C. M. (1963) Behavior therapy, the principles of conditioning, and the treatment of the alcoholic. *Quarterly Journal for the Study of Alcoholism,* 24, 511-529.

Freedman, A. M., Kaplan, H. I., & Sadock, B. J. (1975) *Comprehensive Textbook of Psychiatry — II.* Baltimore: Williams & Wilkins.

Gendreau, P. (1995) The principles of effective intervention with offenders. In: A. Harland (Ed.) *What Works in Community Corrections,* Thousand Oaks, CA: Sage.

Gilliland, B. E., James, R. K., & Bowman, J. T. (1994) *Theories and Strategies in Counseling and Psychotherapy.* Needham Heights, MA: Allyn & Bacon.

Glasser, W. (1961) *Mental Health or Mental Illness?* New York: Harper & Row.

Glasser, W. (1965) *Reality Therapy.* New York: Harper & Row.

Glasser, W. (1969) *Schools Without Failure.* New York: Harper & Row.

Glasser, W. (1984) *Control Theory: A New Explanation of How We Control Our Lives.* New York: Harper & Row.

Glasser, W. (1990) *The Control Theory-Reality Therapy Workbook.* Canoga Park, CA: Institute for Reality Therapy.

Goldenberg, H. (1973) *Contemporary Clinical Psychology.* Monterey, CA: Brooks/Cole.

Greenberger, D., & Padesky, C. A. (1995) *Mind Over Mood*. New York: Guilford.

Harris, T. A. (1969) *I'm OK — You're OK*. New York: Harper & Row.

Jones, M. C. (1924) A laboratory study of fear: the case of Peter. *Pediatric Seminar*, 31, 308-315.

Kelly, G. (1955) *The Psychology of Personal Constructs*. New York: Norton.

Lawson, G. W., Ellis, D. C., & Rivers, P. C. (1984) *Essentials of Chemical Dependency Counseling*. Rockville, MD: Aspen Publishers.

Lilenfeld, L. R., & Kaye, W. H. (1996) The link between alcoholism and eating disorders. *Alcohol Health & Research World*, 20, 94-99.

Little, G. L. (1992) *Cognitive-Behavioral Treatments Applied To Substance Abusers*. Memphis: Eagle Wing Books, Inc.

Little, G. L. (1997a) *Psychopharmacology: Basics for Counselors*. Memphis: Advanced Training Associates.

Little, G. L. (1997b) *Staying Quit: A Cognitive-Behavioral Approach to Relapse Prevention*. Memphis: Advanced Training Associates.

Little, G. L. (1996) Relapse Prevention: an overview. *Focus*, 2.

Little, G. L., & Robinson, K. D. (1986) *How To Escape Your Prison*. Memphis: Eagle Wing Books, Inc.

Little, G. L., & Robinson, K. D. (1988) Moral Reconation Therapy: a systematic, step-by-step treatment system for treatment resistant clients. *Psychological Reports*, 62, 135-151.

Little, G. L., & Robinson, K. D. (1991) *Character Development*

Through Will Power and Self-discipline. Memphis: Eagle Wing Books, Inc.

Little, G. L., & Robinson, K. D. (1994) *Family Support: Responsibly Fulfilling A Life's Obligation.* Memphis: Eagle Wing Books, Inc.

Little, G. L., & Robinson, K. D. (1994) *Job Readiness: A Cognitive-Behavioral Workbook.* Memphis: Eagle Wing Books, Inc.

Little, G. L., & Robinson, K. D. (1995a) *Bringing Peace To Relationships.* Memphis: Eagle Wing Books, Inc.

Little, G. L., & Robinson, K. D. (1995b) *Parenting and Family Values: A Cognitive-Behavioral MRT® Workbook.* Memphis: Eagle Wing Books, Inc.

Little, G. L., & Robinson, K. D. (1997) *Coping With Anger: A Cognitive-Behavioral Workbook.* Memphis: Eagle Wing Books, Inc.

Little, G. L., & Robinson, K. D. (1997) *Understanding and Treating Antisocial Personality Disorder: Criminals, Chemical Abusers, & Batterers.* Memphis: Eagle Wing Books, Inc.

Little, G. L., Robinson, K. D., Burnette, K. D., & Swan, E. S. (1996) Review of outcome data with MRT®: seven year recidivism results. *Cognitive-Behavioral Treatment Review*, 5 (1), 1-7.

Marks, S. J., Daroff, L. H., & Granick, S. (1985) Basic Individual Counseling for Drug Abusers. In: *Treatment Services for Adolescent Substance Abusers.* Washington, D.C.: NIDA.

Mathias, R. Specialized approach shows promise for treating antisocial drug abuse patients. *NIDA Notes*, Sept/Oct, 10-11; 14.

Meador, B. D. (1973) Client-centered therapy. In: *Current Psychotherapies.* R. Corsini (Ed.) Itasca, IL: Peacock.

Meichenbaum, D. H. (1977) *Cognitive-Behavior Modification: An Integrative Approach.* New York: Plenum.

Meichenbaum, D. H. (1996) *Mixed Anxiety and Depression: A Cognitive-Behavioral Approach.* New York: Newbridge Prof. Progs.

Minneapolis-St Paul *Press Journal* (November 9, 1993) Treatment programs not always successful, p. 8D.

Moore, T. V. (1939) *Cognitive Psychology.* New York: Lippincott.

Morosco, T. E., & Baer, P. E. (1970) Avoidance conditioning of alcoholics. In: R. Ulrich, et. al. (Eds.) *Control of Human Behavior: From Cure to Prevention.* Glenview, IL: Scott Foresman.

Myers, D. (1992) *Psychology,* NY: Worth Publ.

Palmer, T. (1993) *Programmatic and Nonprogrammatic Aspects of Successful Intervention.* LaCrosse, WI: Intl. Assoc. of Residential and Community Alternatives.

Pavlov, I. P. (1927) *Conditioned Reflexes.* London: Oxford Univ. Press.

Pennington, L. A., & Berg, I. A. (1954) *An Introduction to Clinical Psychology.* New York: Ronald Press.

Perls, F. (1947) *Ego, Hunger, and Aggression.* London: Allen & Unwin.

Perls, F. (1969) *Gestalt Therapy Verbatim.* Moab, UT: Real People Press.

Perls, F., Hefferline, R., & Goodman, P. (1951) *Gestalt Therapy: Excitement and Growth in the Human Personality.* New York: Dell Books.

Regier, D. A., Farmer, M. E., Rae, D. S., Locke, B. Z., Keith, S. J., Judd, L. L., & Goodwin, F. K. (1990) Comorbidity of mental disorders with alcohol and other drug abuse. *Journal of the American Medical Association,* 264, 2511-2518.

Rogers, C. R. (1975) Client-centered psychotherapy. In: A. M. Freedman, H. I. Kaplan, & B. J. Sadock (Eds.) *Comprehensive Textbook of Psychiatry — II*. Baltimore: Williams & Wilkins, Pp. 1831-1843.

Rogers, C. R. (1951) *Client-Centered Therapy*. Boston: Houghton-Mifflin.

Rogers, C. R. (1942) *Counseling and Psychotherapy*. Boston: Houghton-Mifflin.

Rogers, C. R. (1961) *On Becoming A Person*. Boston: Houghton-Mifflin.

Ruch, F. L., & Zimbardo, P. G. (1971) *Psychology and Life*. Glenview, IL: Scott, Foresman & Co.

SAMHSA (1996) *Overview of Addiction Treatment Effectiveness*. U. S. Department of Health and Human Services.

Schuckit, M. A. (1996) Alcohol, anxiety, and depressive disorders. *Alcohol Health & Research World*, 20, 81-85.

Strupp, H. H., & Blackwood, G. (1975) Recent methods of psychotherapy. In: A. M. Freedman, H. I. Kaplan, & B. J. Sadock (Eds.) *Comprehensive Textbook of Psychiatry — II*. Baltimore: Williams & Wilkins, Pp. 1909-1920.

Thetford, W., & Schucman, H. (1975) Other psychological personality theories. In: A. M. Freedman, H. I. Kaplan, & B. J. Sadock (Eds.) *Comprehensive Textbook of Psychiatry — II*. Baltimore: Williams & Wilkins, Pp. 687-711.

Thorndike, E. L. (1898) Animal intelligence: an experimental study of the associative processes in animals. *Psychological Monographs*, 2, (8).

Waggonner, A. (1994) Oklahoma's systems approach to treatment through Moral Reconation Therapy. In: *State and Local Programs: Treatment, Rehabilitation, and Education*. Washington, DC: U. S. Bureau of Justice Assistance, Pp. 62-64.

Watson, J. B., & Rayner, R. (1920) Conditioned emotional reactions. *Journal of Experimental Psychology, 3*, 1-14.

Wiens, A. N., & Menustik, C. E. (1983) Treatment outcome and patient characteristics in an aversion therapy program for alcoholism. *American Psychologist, 38*, 1089-1096.

Wolman, B. B. (1973) *Dictionary of Behavioral Science.* New York: Van Nostrand Reinhold.

Wolpe, J. (1958) *Psychotherapy by Reciprocal Inhibition.* Stanford, CA: Stanford Univ. Press.

Woody, G. (1996) The challenge of dual diagnosis. *Alcohol Health & Research World, 20*, 76-80.

Young, H. S. (1986) Practicing RET with lower-class clients. In: W. Dryden & P. Trower (Eds.) *Rational-Emotive Therapy: Recent Developments in Theory and Practice.* Bristol, England: Institute for RET.

INDEX